Foreword

Ortho Biotech Inc. is proud to support and work in partnership with The Susan G. Komen Breast Cancer Foundation in its goal to eradicate breast cancer as a life-threatening disease.

Increasing research, education, screening, treatment, and patient awareness is pivotal to achieving this goal. Nancy Brinker's book, *The Race Is Run One Step at a Time* sensitively portrays how individuals who are informed and resourceful can take an active role in their personal health.

We at Ortho Biotech are deeply committed to efforts that further our understanding of this devastating disease.

The Race Is Run One Step at a Time

My Personal Struggle— and Everywoman's Guide—to Taking Charge of Breast Cancer

NANCY BRINKER
WITH Catherine McEvily Harris
WITH A PREFACE by Dr. Samuel Broder, Director, National Cancer Institute

A FIRESIDE BOOK
Published by Simon & Schuster
NEW YORK, LONDON, TORONTO, SYDNEY, TOKYO, SINGAPORE

FIRESIDE
Simon & Schuster Building
Rockefeller Center
1230 Avenue of the Americas
New York, New York 10020

FIRESIDE and colophon are registered trademarks
of Simon & Schuster Inc.

Designed by Sheree L. Goodman
Manufactured in the United States of America

1 3 5 7 9 10 8 6 4 2

1 3 5 7 9 10 8 6 4 2 Pbk.

Brinker, Nancy.
The race is run one step at a time : my personal struggle and
everywoman's guide to taking charge of breast cancer / Nancy Brinker
with Catherine McEvily Harris : with a preface by Samuel Broder.—
1st Fireside ed.
p. cm.
Reprint. Originally published : New York : Simon & Schuster Inc.
© 1990.
Includes bibliographical references and index.
1. Breast—Cancer—Popular works. I. Harris, Catherine McEvily.
II. Title.
[RC280.B8B73 1991]
362.1'9699449—dc20   91-22160
CIP

ISBN: 0-671-69149-X
ISBN: 0-671-74804-1 Pbk.

To my sister, Susan G. Komen;

To our dear mother, Eleanor Newman Goodman,
and our father, Marvin Goodman, for creating her;

To my husband and son, for helping me keep her memory alive;

And to the Susan G. Komen Breast Cancer Foundation,
through which her spirit will live forever.

Contents

Acknowledgments

Many thanks to my family and friends for their unwavering support. And to my writer, Catherine McEvily Harris, for time, talent, and insight.

Preface

by Dr. Samuel Broder,
   Director, National Cancer Institute

This year approximately 175,000 women will be diagnosed as having breast cancer; approximately 46,000 will die. The search for a cure has been a difficult road. We live in an era of rapid technological changes, and there have been many advances in basic science and clinical practice. But there is still much to learn. Breast cancer patients with a practical knowledge of the disease have a great advantage.

The Race Is Run One Step at a Time will make the road considerably easier—at least easy enough to follow. Scientists and physicians often forget they are speaking to people unacquainted with cancer terminology. This book makes the medical jargon clear and meaningful.

Nancy Brinker's book is not intended for women alone, but for everyone. Breast cancer touches the lives of all of us. This important volume gives women, and the men and children who love and care about them, a starting point—a compass with which they can begin their race to obtain information. In telling her personal story, Brinker teaches by example, and, in outlining her knowledge, she provides a model for the informed patient.

Bench science will never be adequately transferred to the clinic without a population of informed patients. An educated population is the best ally of physicians dedicated to preventing, diagnosing, and treating breast cancer.

Nancy Brinker is driven to do something about this disease. She founded the Komen Foundation—an organization that supports research and training, and is making a real difference—to honor a sister who died of breast cancer. During the course of Brinker's crusade, the disease eventually threatened her own life. With the establishment of the Komen Foundation

11

she turned her personal battle with cancer into a public mission. With the publication of this book, Nancy Brinker is making yet another important contribution.

Breast cancer is an exceedingly high priority of the National Cancer Institute. Through research, we have learned how certain hormones or growth factors can lead to abnormal growth patterns, ultimately contributing to the development of cancer. We now know about special genes (oncogenes) that may directly contribute to cancer. A newer class of genes (suppressor genes) can prevent the malignant state to begin with. As we proceed, this kind of research will make a tremendous difference in locating a cure, but there is also much we can do now to battle the disease. Regular mammograms and clinical exams can have great success in detecting and curing breast cancer. New approaches to surgery and follow-up chemotherapy or hormonal therapy can make a big difference in a woman's survival and in the quality of her life. Multidisciplinary cooperation can make breast cancer treatment a team effort. Better information services, such as the Physicians Data Query (PDQ) system can provide up-to-the-minute information for physicians and surgeons. And information services for the general public can be enormously effective.

The first step, however, begins with the patient and her family. That's what this book is all about.

Introduction

Nothing in life is to be feared.
It is only to be understood.

—MADAME CURIE

The last thing in the world I ever thought I'd do was write a book. The truth is, I never thought I could sit still long enough to complete one. I would never have imagined myself having so much to say on any one particular subject.

Of course, I never imagined I'd be living my life without the company of my sister, Susan Goodman Komen. Growing up in Peoria, Illinois, Suzy and I were filled with childhood dreams. Our dreams were always very different, but that didn't seem to matter because we also had many things in common. We spent endless hours discussing in intricate detail the paths our lives were likely to take. Suzy's always pertained to having a handsome husband, a family, and a home in Peoria while mine took on a much grander vision. I wanted all of the above and more. I can remember as far back as when I was three years old plotting and scheming ways to get *out* of Peoria. I wanted more excitement and stimulation than any hometown could offer.

Even as a little girl I always had high aspirations. Leading a quiet, sedentary life was not an option—I had to see the world. I had no way of knowing what a cataclysmic series of events would have to take place before that vision would become reality.

Regardless of how our lives were to differ, Suzy and I always planned to take care of our parents together when the time came, share a room in the "old folks home" one day, and compare stories about our husbands, kids, and grandchildren. It never dawned on me that things could turn out so differently. No, I must admit that not one of our many childhood dreams included breast cancer. Even I, with the most vivid of imaginations, never thought about what it would be like to spend three years watching this disease slowly and painfully suck the life out of my best friend. Not once did I fantasize about what it would be like to hear those dreaded words, "It's cancer," referring to my own breast. Nor did I think for a minute that I'd start a national foundation for breast cancer research in my sister's memory.

As all too often happens in the game of life, I was dealt an unexpected hand of cards. God knows, I'm not the first woman to experience such a hand. I'm not even the first woman to put her story on paper. There have been others before me who have bravely told their stories to the world and were far more prolific than I.

So, why am I doing this? What would make a person share such painful and intimate details of her life? Allow me to offer a statistic that says it all:

> During the ten years of the Vietnam War,
> 58,000 men and women died.
> During that same ten-year period,
> 330,000 women died of breast cancer.

Breast cancer is our country's number-two killer of women.

Thirty years ago, one out of twenty women was diagnosed with the disease. Today the figure has grown to one in nine and the number is still growing. It is a disease that strikes women in the prime of their most productive years of life, often attacking its victims between the ages of thirty and fifty. It is also a disease that tears into the depths of a woman's soul and threatens what she often cherishes most, her femininity and her self-image. Today, a woman over thirty-five is at the forefront of an exciting era. She's at a new pinnacle in terms of career, family, romance, and sexuality. Often she is starting over in one or more of these areas. Breast cancer threatens to take it all away. And what it leaves in its place is a woman with a disease that is hard to discuss, difficult to endure, and nearly impossible to prevent.

Fifty years ago, when a person was diagnosed with breast cancer it meant the worst. Gloom and doom hovered over that person like a dark rain cloud. And, whether it was mentioned aloud or not, a slow and painful death was almost always envisioned by all. Fortunately, times have changed. No one has to give in to breast cancer anymore or assume that it will eventually be the victor. Nor should one assume that engaging in battle with breast cancer will permanently devalue her quality of life. I have personally witnessed the best and worst of the situation. My sister died a slow and painful death. She was not educated about the disease and neither were the people on whom she relied most. Because of Suzy's death and my promise to her on her deathbed, I have made it a point to learn everything I can about breast cancer. I'm still learning every day.

When cancer was discovered in my own breast, of course I was frightened. I cried and experienced all of the reactions you would expect of a woman diagnosed with a life-threatening disease. But I had an advantage Suzy didn't have—an advantage you'll have too: I had a pretty good idea what my options were and knew where to go for the answers I was missing. I assembled what I affectionately refer to as my "A Team" of experts and together we met the disease head on. The point I want to make is this: after having my breast removed, receiving high doses of chemotherapy, and undergoing reconstructive surgery, my life is fuller and more active than ever before. It has not deteriorated one bit. I work out every day, play polo three times a week, work full-time for the Susan G. Komen Breast Cancer Foundation which I founded after Suzy's death, and keep a very full social calendar—none of which is as strenuous as keeping up with my eighteen-year-old son. The two major differences in my life now compared to before I had cancer are that today I am much busier and I appreciate the value of good health as never before. I am telling you this because I want you to know what I know. Even if you find yourself diagnosed with breast cancer, it does not have to mean the end of the world. Dealing with this disease requires a plan of action. A good football team maps out its winning strategy. So should you. But before you can do that, you must know something about the game.

So far, there is no cure. But there *is* hope. When breast cancer is detected in its earliest stages, there is a 95 percent survival rate. My cancer was detected early; my sister's was not. I had the opportunity to marshal my possibilities; my sister did not. I am living a full and happy life with a son and a husband who are more precious to me than anything in the world. My sister left behind two young children, a very lonely husband, two heartbroken parents, many wonderful friends, and me.

My object is not to frighten you with statistics on breast cancer—quite the contrary. Suzy was frightened, so frightened that her fear paralyzed her judgment. She is dead. This is not to say my sister's death could have been prevented. Ten percent of all breast cancers are so aggressive and grow so fast they simply *outsmart* all forms of treatment, and that very well may have been the case with Suzy's. But I believe in my heart that had all of us been better informed about the facts, had we known enough to try all the options available, her life might have been prolonged, if not saved. Those precious few years would have provided her two children with more of the nurturing they so desperately needed. The prospect of discovering cancer in yourself or someone you love is one of the most terrifying feelings imaginable. But believe me when I tell you that you are better off if you feel anger along with the terror. Cancer is one of those enemies that needs to be dealt with immediately. Anger, focused positively, provides you with strength.

The purpose of writing this book is to empower you by helping you to deal with the considerable amount of information you *need* to know in order to stand a fighting chance against breast cancer. I have learned a great deal in the past twelve years. God knows, the opportunity has presented itself. My sister's life was taken by breast cancer, and my own life was threatened by the same disease. Now breast cancer is my career. The knowledge I've accumulated wasn't part of my plan. It was born from the necessity of dealing with the hand of cards I was dealt. Unfortunately, I couldn't throw my hand in—you can't either. I don't believe, however, that the only way to learn important lessons in life is by making your own mistakes. The most powerful gift of the written word is its ability to reach out and teach those who may follow an already traveled path. Learn from my mistakes and the mistakes of my family. Learn from our triumphs, too. I wasn't born with any phenomenal gifts. I am just a regular woman who grew up in midwestern America. I do not presume to pose as a medical authority. But what I have found in my quest for knowledge is that the dark, mysterious picture which is automatically conjured up in many minds by the word *science* is not that dark and not that mysterious. It is a matter of deciphering the code, as it were, and learning the language. Once I understood what all those pathologists, radiologists, oncologists, and surgeons were talking about, I was able to think more clearly and make intelligent decisions about my own cancer.

I have structured the book into two parts. In Part One, I will tell you what happened to Suzy and me. The story may be, at times, painful to read; I know it was painful to write. We were two sisters with the same disease. One of us lived; one of us died. We each handled our breast cancer very differently, both medically and mentally. In those differences lies the theme of this book. I fought my illness with everything I had. My sister didn't have my knowledge or experience. She couldn't have fought the same way I did.

Part Two is directed to you, the reader. I will take you through what is thought to be the basics. There is a lot to know about the breasts, not just about breast cancer but about benign breast disease and how the breasts function normally. If you have a true sense of how your body works without a problem, you will then develop a sort of *sixth sense* which will make you acutely aware should anything out of the ordinary occur. As we delve into the specifics of the disease itself, I will try to give you the information you'll need most in order to combat breast cancer. The truth, as I know it, is that the only way to overcome an obstacle in life is to follow a well-charted plan. We'll talk about treatment, old and new, both surgical and nonsurgical. Things are changing every day in the world of medicine. We'll also talk about what's on the horizon in terms of forthcoming research and what is being done to help overcome the emotional aspects of this very personal and intimate disease. And, finally, we'll talk about what little is known about the causes of breast cancer and the preventive measures assumed at this time.

Until a cure is found, we must fight with the only weapon we have— knowledge. No, I am not a doctor, but I can assist you in finding one. I would like to help you put together your own "A Team" of experts. And on this team, it will be up to you to call the shots. We all have to take responsibility for our own bodies. We can solicit the help of the finest experts in the country, but the final choices have to be our own. We can't make wise choices without valid information. For far too long the majority of information has been left in the hands of men. Breast cancer is largely a women's disease (one percent of all diagnosed cases of breast cancer are found in men), yet it is mostly men on whom we depend for research and treatment. I often wonder just how much closer we'd be to finding a cure if the statistics were as high on breast cancer cases diagnosed in men as they are in women. If I am successful in my purpose for writing this book, by the time you finish the last page you will have more knowledge and feel better armed against this formidable opponent. Ultimately, you will have the ability to make informed decisions about your own health and well-being.

Through the Susan G. Komen Breast Cancer Foundation I have been able to keep my sister's memory alive. The women and men who have become cherished members of our cause have helped, each in his or her own way, to fill the vast void in my heart left by her death. Suzy didn't want anyone to suffer the way she did. I don't either. The good news is . . . you may not have to.

PART ONE:

My Sister and I

Suzy's Story

The first time I can remember hearing the words *breast cancer* was back in 1956. I was ten years old and living in Peoria, Illinois, with my parents, Eleanor and Marvin Goodman, and my older sister, Susan. Our home was on a quiet, tree-lined street in a peaceful neighborhood where every neighbor was a friend, much like a scene right out of *Father Knows Best*. It was a traditional life and the rules were clearly laid out. Dinner was served on a white tablecloth and good manners were mandatory. Mealtime was family time in the Goodman household and that meant no interruptions. No boyfriends, no phone calls—no nothing. Dad was the family leader and authoritarian, of that there was no doubt. Although we always felt loved, he was a very strict man who demanded respect. It was this discipline that gave us our structure and me my drive. It would hurt his feelings terribly if I said I thought he loved Suzy more, but their relationship *was* different. Suzy was his first child and born a bit premature. She was a meeker and milder child, not to mention a lot smaller than me. He idolized little Suzy and in his eyes she could do no wrong. The truth of the matter is, she *did* no wrong. I, on the other hand, started out on the wrong foot from the beginning. I was supposed to be a boy. I weighed in at over a hundred pounds in second grade and had all the grace and poise of a baby elephant. I wasn't nearly as cuddly as my sister, but I had a quick, curious mind. Dad simply expected more from me. Looking back now, I'm grateful for being taught to push harder, but back then it was sometimes hard to swallow.

My mother has always been a woman of amazing patience, kindness, and inner strength. She allowed my father to "run" the family, yet she was the one who knew all our secrets, kept all our confidences. When some-

21

thing needed to be done, we depended on her for results. And she never let us down. Mom was a great mediator between my father and everyone else. She was and still is the world's best peacekeeper. She ran the Girl Scouts in Peoria, was a tireless charity volunteer, never missed a PTA meeting, was usually in the kitchen baking cookies when Suzy and I came home from school, and always had dinner waiting for my father at the end of each day. And she did it all with a smile on her face. But my mother's finest gift to the world is her ability to find the humor in any situation.

Suzy and I were unable to suppress squeals of joy when we were informed one night at dinner that we were going to visit our favorite aunt, Rose, all the way in New York City. Since Suzy was thirteen, Mom and Dad felt we were old enough to make the trip by plane to the big city by ourselves. To me, it was to be an exciting adventure, never mind the fact that our parents would put us safely on the plane and Aunt Rose would be waiting at the other end to pick us up.

Anyway, that night after dinner my mother came into our bedroom while we were dutifully doing our homework and told us she had something to talk to us about. She wanted to remind us that although Aunt Rose was feeling great and looked good, she had been very sick with breast cancer and had had an operation called a mastectomy. Suzy quickly jumped in and told Mom we both knew about the operation and she didn't need to explain the details of Aunt Rose's surgery. In the back of my mind I had an idea what a mastectomy was, but I could tell, even then, that the subject was uncomfortable for Suzy—so I didn't ask any questions. Any subject with even so much as a hint of violence, pain, or mutilation would upset her terribly. I remember when Suzy's stallion was being gelded, she ran away screaming with her hands over her face while I sat up in a nearby tree and, although I winced and covered my eyes, through parted fingers I watched the whole thing with great interest.

By the time we saw Aunt Rose, so ebullient and full of life, laughing and flirting with her new husband (her fourth), all thoughts that she had once been sick passed completely from our minds. We listened intently while Rose told of her exotic safari in Africa. Oh, how I admired this woman. She did anything she wanted to do, any time she wanted to do it. She was independent and free-spirited and I wanted to be just like her. Suzy admired her too, but for different reasons. She saw in Aunt Rose the epitome of femininity. And she was right. Aunt Rose was truly glamorous. She entered and exited every room just like Loretta Young, with a chiffon scarf floating through the air. Her clothes were always beautiful and her perfume wafted behind her in a way that left her on your mind long after she had gone. And she did have a way with men! She knew how to get men to do anything and everything she wanted them to do, and she did it by making those men feel as if they were the most important and wonderful thing in her life.

On our third night in New York, something happened that would have a lasting effect on Suzy and me. Aunt Rose had taken us shopping, skating, and to the theater. We had had a long day and Suzy and I were simply exhausted. As sometimes happens when two sisters are both tired, Suzy and I got into a little squabble before bedtime. Whatever the argument was about we just couldn't seem to resolve it between ourselves this time, so Suzy marched in to discuss the matter with Aunt Rose. All of a sudden Suzy came tearing back into our room in a hysterical frenzy. I had never seen her so upset. She looked terrified. When I finally got her to calm down long enough to tell me what was wrong, she reported that she had gone into Aunt Rose's room without knocking and had accidentally seen the scars on her chest. She said they were terribly gruesome and she couldn't understand how Aunt Rose had lived through such mutilation. Naturally, I had to check out the situation for myself. So I tiptoed back to Aunt Rose's room and quietly opened the door to get a quick peek. Well, Suzy wasn't kidding. Not only were the scars severe, but her chest looked concave and burned from high-voltage cobalt treatments. I could even faintly see her heart beating through thin, purple skin. Aunt Rose had had what is known as a Halsted radical mastectomy on her left side. Although the procedure is rarely done today, it was considered common treatment for breast cancer for nearly a hundred years and was certainly common back then in 1956. The Halsted radical removes not only the breast but all of the underarm lymph nodes, the chest muscles, and some additional fat and skin. The truth is, her particular operation *was* unattractive. I have since learned more about the procedure and realize that hers was poorly done. But, as I softly closed the door and began to walk back to Suzy, I heard Aunt Rose singing happily to her husband. I decided Aunt Rose didn't need my sympathy. Aunt Rose was living a fuller, richer, more exciting life than anyone else I knew. If her mastectomy didn't bother her, why should it bother me? But Suzy never got over it. The memory of Aunt Rose's chest haunted her forever.

As we got older, Suzy and I became just about as close as two sisters can get. Suzy was the perfect older sister. She was beautiful and kind and loving, not only to me but to everyone. There was a goodness and gen-

(1)Suzy, Dad (Marvin Goodman), and me, 1952.

(2)With Suzy and Mother (Ellie Goodman), and Aunt Rose and her husband whom she married after her radical mastectomy.

tleness about my sister that went unnoticed by no one. She was the star of our hometown of Peoria, the high school homecoming queen, the college beauty queen. She was everyone's darling and I don't think there was a soul who ever met her who didn't fall in love with her—men, women, and children alike. I worshiped Suzy and used to follow her around everywhere. She never seemed to mind. If she did, she never showed it. I, on the other hand, was bigger, heavier, and taller than most of my friends *and* her friends. I developed my own way of getting attention. I was a tomboy and a mischief-maker and delighted in nothing more than spending hours galloping around on horseback. Suzy tried desperately to teach me about all the pretty things in life: how to fix my hair, apply makeup, and coordinate my wardrobe. None of it seemed to work. I was still a big, sort of clumsy girl with two left feet. The boys didn't know I was alive, except that I was Susan Goodman's younger, "bookish" sister. The only frustration we ever had with each other was that it bothered me that Suzy seemed content to stay right where she was just as it bothered her to constantly see the discontent in my eyes.

Suzy came back to Peoria when she graduated from college and got a job modeling locally. Eventually, she married her college sweetheart, Stan Komen. Stan and Suzy had a very good marriage. Although they were unable to have children of their own, they soon adopted two beautiful babies, Scott and Stephanie. Suzy had everything she wanted: a loving husband and a family of her own.

College, for me, was the first time I felt I belonged anywhere. At the University of Illinois, the baby fat came off as did the braces. I was active in many school projects and finally began to have confidence in myself. I felt independent and responsible and ready to take on the world. After graduating, I packed up my bags and moved to Dallas, home of my father's older sister, Aunt Ruth. As a child, I had spent many vacations in Texas and often dreamed of one day living amid the wide open ranchland. When Dad finally agreed to the move, or at least realized he couldn't stop me, he made it clear that I would have to support myself.

So I walked into Neiman Marcus and told the personnel director my situation. "Look," I said, "my parents are not happy about my being in Texas. I need a job, and I need a good one." I started as an executive trainee and worked up to an assistant couture buyer. It was at Neiman Marcus that I met my first husband. The marriage, by all counts, was a mistake, except for one wonderful miracle—my son, Eric.

Although we were separated by distance, Suzy and I spoke every day by phone in the late afternoon. Our daily conversations were something I grew to depend on and cherish. She kept me up-to-date on what was happening in Peoria and I filled her in on my life in Dallas. We discussed our children, our husbands, and our careers at great length. Suzy's calm, kind-hearted way was a perfect contrast to my frantic, impatient nature. In a way, I was her third child and she was my second mother. Above all, we made each other laugh.

It was about this time that Suzy and I became aware we both had a common and nonthreatening condition called fibrocystic disease. This is a lumpiness in the breast caused by the breast's response to hormonal levels as they change from month to month. Lumpy, or cystic, breasts are often accompanied by pain or tenderness that fluctuates with the menstrual cycle, becoming more noticeable and painful just before your period begins. Fibrocystic disease is by far the most frequently occurring breast disorder and nearly all women's breasts develop some degree of this condition at one time or another. We will talk about fibrocystic disease in more detail in Chapter 3, but the point I want to make now is that neither Suzy nor I was concerned in the least about our condition. Occasionally, Suzy's doctor would perform what is called a needle aspiration. Using a needle and syringe to withdraw fluid or a small amount of tissue from a breast lump can show whether that lump is a fluid-filled cyst or a solid mass. Hers were fluid-filled cysts and by puncturing the lump with a needle, the mass drained and disappeared. Regardless of how it sounds, this procedure was, again, nothing that caused her alarm. Our doctors assured us that eight out of ten lumps were not dangerous in any way and that we had nothing to worry about. Besides, we both felt young and invincible.

As if it were yesterday, I can remember the phone call I received from Suzy one Tuesday afternoon. Her doctor had found a lump that was not a cyst. He recommended a biopsy. A biopsy is the surgical removal and microscopic examination of tissue to see if cancer cells are present. Now, you must understand that my sister was the most nurturing, loving woman in the world. She took it upon herself to help everyone who crossed her path. And, by force of habit, we not only allowed her to comfort us when we needed it, we grew to depend on it. Hearing uneasiness in her voice, as much as she tried to hide it, was unnatural. And it frightened me. Of course, my parents and I tried to make light of the situation and tell Suzy we were sure that everything would be fine. But, to be honest, we weren't sure at all. Not at all. And although none of us mentioned it, the memory of Aunt Rose had been brought back to life vividly in all our minds.

(3)Me (right) with my best friend, Suzy, 1975.

I decided to fly home to Peoria. Suzy said it wasn't necessary, that she would call me when they found out the results. I insisted on coming anyway, saying that I wanted to be there for the celebration when the tests came back negative. But when I got off the plane, my father was waiting there alone with an expression on his face I will never forget. He didn't have to say a word. *At the age of thirty-three, Suzy had breast cancer.*

What happened from this point on is still difficult for me to talk about because I am so much more knowledgeable on the subject today. *If I had only known then what I know now.*

The truth of the matter is that growing up in the small town of Peoria, our family had been treated our whole lives by one doctor. He was a nice man and a fine physician, and we relied on him for all of our childhood illnesses. He was probably the last of the kind, older doctors who still made house calls and was a friend not only to us, but to everyone he treated. Suzy trusted him with her cancer the same way she trusted him with her measles. *Mistake number one.* None of us knew enough to inquire about seeking information from a major cancer center near our town or from a group of physicians associated with one in Peoria. He was our doctor. Period.

The most difficult concept to grasp about cancer, I think, is the fact that when it is first detected the patient usually feels just fine. There is rarely any pain associated with breast cancer in its early stages. So when you are told you've got a life-threatening disease, and the treatment sounds more heinous than the thought of a little lump in the breast, it is understandable that a woman uneducated about cancer might opt for no treatment at all. Such was the case with Suzy. My sister was terrified, naturally, but adamant against having a mastectomy. She wasn't vain in a negative sense; she was just extremely feminine and enjoyed every part of being a woman. That included having breasts. Two of them.

Our family doctor called in a surgeon to review Suzy's case. It is important, if you are to learn from our mistakes, that I tell you a little bit about this surgeon. He was very handsome, very suave, and seemed very self-confident. He told us that her cancer was a medullary carcinoma and there were no lymph nodes involved. I will go into more detail about this medical terminology later on, but briefly what I understood him to mean was that in his opinion her cancer had not spread or metastasized to other parts of her body. According to Suzy, this surgeon—I will refer to him as Dr. Smith (not his real name)—told Suzy he could cure her. Even the most respected cancer experts in the country (which Dr. Smith was certainly not) talk about recovery in terms of surviving cancer or remission. They refrain from using the word *cure* because cancer can recur.

But that, of course, is exactly what Suzy wanted to hear, and who could blame her? Like many women, and for that matter men too, Suzy was of the frame of mind that the doctor was always right. She believed in Dr. Smith without question, and when he smiled at her and said everything would be fine, she willingly gave herself up to this man. Suzy really didn't want to know everything there was to know about the disease, she just wanted him to make her better. She wanted not to be frightened anymore, she wanted to look normal, and she wanted to go back to being a healthy wife and mother to her children.

Dr. Smith suggested performing a subcutaneous mastectomy, a procedure in which the outside of the breast is left intact but an incision is made and the breast tissue is removed. He would then do an implant ten days later. She would be left with a small scar but no more cancer. Suzy felt it was her best option. Nor was she referred to an oncologist—a cancer specialist—for a second opinion. The year was 1977 and although cancer treatments weren't nearly as sophisticated as they are today we wish she had been offered the chance to participate in a clinical trial at a major comprehensive cancer center. A clinical trial is an experimental study conducted with cancer patients, usually to evaluate a new treatment. Each study is designed to answer specific scientific questions. A patient is randomly assigned to one of several treatments with the scientific goals being to measure the success of one over the other. At that time, they would sometimes compare a patient receiving a certain formula of drugs with a patient receiving no drugs at all. And because the assignments were random, there was always the chance she would have been put in a group without drugs, but at least she would have been part of a closely monitored study conducted by doctors at a comprehensive cancer center.

The rest of us tried very hard among ourselves to figure out what was best for her. But at that time, we were certainly no experts. Suzy was very upset and Stan wanted to keep her calm, so he went along with what she wanted. My mother instinctively had a lot of questions, but was afraid to push too hard, fearing Suzy might decide to do nothing rather than go for more intense treatment. My father was devastated and did not know where to turn or what to do. It was very sad. I, being the rebel, wanted Suzy to get out of Peoria and have a second opinion at a comprehensive cancer center. To me, both our family doctor and Dr. Smith, while their intentions were good, lacked the sophistication and exposure that can only be found through years of concentrated study in a given field. Their attention had been too diversified, treating everything from chicken pox to appendectomies. These are normal and admirable credentials in small town physicians, but in my opinion, not good enough for my sister's condition at that time. I wanted Suzy to have the best, I wanted her to come to Texas. But she wanted to stay in Peoria where she was comfortable and loved. And that is exactly what she did.

After Suzy's surgery, my parents, Stan, and I were all at the hospital anxiously awaiting the results. Dr. Smith walked confidently in the room and said, "You can relax; we got it all. I believe she's cured." My heart sank because I knew enough to know that *cure* is a very difficult word to use in reference to cancer. If it is used at all, it is more likely to be spoken after a five-year period has passed without a recurrence.

Let me set the record straight about Suzy's doctors: neither of them had anything but good intentions, nor did they want anything less than good health for her. Both of these doctors loved my sister and wanted nothing more than to see her well. And she loved them. Suzy felt that the better she knew her doctors, the closer the doctor/patient relationship, the better the prognosis. She felt that because these doctors were her *friends*, they wouldn't let her down. They *couldn't* let her down because friends don't do that to each other. Aside from radiation, I don't remember other treatment or adjuvant therapy being suggested. Nowadays it is common to perform additional tests such as bone scans, liver scans or CAT scans to determine whether cancer has metasticized.

For the next five months or so, Suzy felt pretty good. She was convinced she was cured. When I suggested she secure a second opinion just to be sure, she became very sensitive. After all, her doctor had told her she was fine. I was back in Dallas, having my own problems dealing with a failing marriage. Suzy didn't want to talk about her illness so, God bless her, she spent hours on the phone each day counseling me. I was concerned because Suzy had a shallow cough that wouldn't go away and she really didn't seem to have her energy back. She was cheerful and happy, but that old zing and sparkle just wasn't there. I didn't dare suggest that she was still sick. How could I, when Suzy was so optimistic? Quietly, I worried.

Before six months had gone by, our worst nightmare became a reality. Suzy found another lump. This time it was under her arm. Despite everyone's optimism her cancer had spread.

I wanted to take Suzy to the M.D. Anderson Cancer Center in Houston because through my contacts in Dallas, I had learned this facility was one of the most comprehensive cancer centers in the country. Suzy wasn't familiar with M.D. Anderson, but she knew about the Mayo Clinic so that's where she went next. It was at Mayo where we learned that her cancer had metastasized (spread) to her lung and under her arm. There was a tumor the size of a quarter in the upper part of her right lung and suspicious shadows elsewhere. Their recommendation was thirty days of radiation and then to "watch it." Well I, for one, was tired of "watching." I wanted to see some results.

Terror, rage, sadness, and above all, a feeling of complete and utter helplessness invaded me. Why was this happening to Suzy, of all people? What in the hell had she ever done to deserve to be so sick and so frightened? Although no one said anything aloud, we all knew my sister was now fighting for her life. *And it all happened so quickly.* She tried to keep up a brave front and would often talk of plans for the future.

A major turning point in Suzy's struggle for survival came from a surprising source, Mrs. Betty Ford. The year was 1978 and Mrs. Ford had finished a successful bout with breast cancer as First Lady. The whole country was shocked and saddened with the news of her breast cancer and mastectomy. Her bravery touched a place inside of Suzy that none of us could possibly understand because we hadn't gone through it ourselves. In Betty Ford, my sister found new strength. "Nan," she said, "if Mrs. Ford can admit she has breast cancer and tell the whole world she intends to fight it, well then so can I." The doctors at Mayo suggested Suzy have radiation therapy, which is a treatment using high-energy rays to damage (burn) cancer cells and stop them from growing. She did have the radiation but it was not successful in slowing her disease. The cancer was out of control and there wasn't a damn thing we could do about it. But we had to try. Thank goodness, Suzy's plastic surgeon in Peoria suggested she try M.D. Anderson. I guess there is something about hearing advice from a nonfamily member that allows it to sink in. It didn't matter; I was thrilled she had decided to give Houston a try.

Through contacts I had made when helping with a charity benefit for M.D. Anderson, I was able to get Suzy an appointment with an oncologist (a doctor who specializes in the treatment of cancer) by the name of George Blumenschein. It is probably unfair for me to single out one man when there were so many men and women who tried desperately to save my sister's life. But Dr. Blumenschein represented an attitude and spirit in medicine that we had not seen up until this point. Before coming to M.D. Anderson, her treatment had always been unilateral, meaning one doctor and one patient. Now, for the first time, Suzy was part of a team. *Dr. Blumenschein and his associates made Suzy a partner in every decision.* They were completely and totally honest with her and all of us about her condition. When Suzy arrived in Houston, she was a Stage IV cancer patient. This means that the disease had spread to other organs in her body and was still growing. It is a very critical situation. Dr. Blumenschein threw the book at her, in a sense. He not only told her everything, but he showed her the results of her tests. Rather than speak to Suzy in terms like "I will do this" or "I will do that," he said "We can do this" or "Let's try that." He told Suzy exactly what her chances of survival were and what *they* had to do in order to fight this cancer. He said, "Susan, we will do everything we can to try to save you, but we can't do it without your help and cooperation." Suzy was not only *allowed* to ask questions, she was *encouraged* to do so.

Dr. Blumenschein's approach to the disease was an aggressive one. After recommending removing the lesion from her lung, he told Suzy that she had a twenty-five percent chance of survival, but that if she wouldn't give up, *he* wouldn't give up. He wanted to put her in a treatment protocol (that is, a combination of drugs—in this case the combination was being tested in a clinical trial) at M.D. Anderson and promised her that if one didn't work he would try another. Thus began a saga of intense chemotherapy. Chemotherapy is usually a combination of several drugs given together, delivered into the patient's bloodstream, that are highly toxic to fast-growing cells. The problem with chemotherapy is that it doesn't know the difference between the good guys and the bad guys, so a lot of important healthy cells are killed in the process, including the cells of the stomach lining and hair roots. Chemotherapy is often accompanied by nausea, mouth sores, hair thinning, and sometimes total hair loss, depending on the type used. Suzy experienced all of that and more. Everyone given chemotherapy is warned that a side effect is hair loss, but nothing can prepare a woman for the shock and embarrassment of baldness. She bore up under the strain with all the dignity and grace she could manage, although I know she was devastated. Little did I know that even then, my sister was teaching me.

Her partnership with George Blumenschein gave Suzy focus. Because chemotherapy and radiation are given in cycles so that a patient can have alternate periods of treatment and rest, she was able to come home and spend time with her family between trips to Houston. While at home she tried to live as normal a life as possible, with the exception of a surgery to remove a small portion of her right lung where the cancer had invaded. She continued her charity work and spent long afternoons at the hospital in Peoria sitting with terminally ill patients. To this day I hear from the families of the people Suzy sat with. She even continued her modeling when she felt up to it, sporting a new look with a short-cut wig. She had sores in her mouth from all the medication, her arm was painful and swollen from lymphedema, and she had put on weight from the steroids used to slow her cancer, but Suzy still looked beautiful. I don't think I was ever more proud of my sister.

My mother, Stan, and I tried our best to be with her while she was in Houston. If we all couldn't be there together, one of us would be there at all times. She never went alone. There is a hotel apartment across the street from the medical center where patients can stay during their courses of chemotherapy and radiation. Besides being a lot less expensive than staying every night in the hospital, it gives the patient a little bit of freedom. On nights when Suzy wasn't feeling too sick, we were able to get out to eat or catch a movie. She was able to receive her second course of chemotherapy through what is called a Gershon or subclavian catheter. For her, it was a more comfortable way of receiving the drugs. The catheter is placed in a vein just above the clavicle and remains there throughout the course. A small battery-operated pump, which is carried by the patient either around the shoulder or on a belt, automatically delivers the chemo into the vein. You see, she couldn't receive the chemotherapy in the arm on the side of her surgery; there is too high a risk of infection. In the other arm, Suzy's veins had already collapsed from the continual abuse of so many needles.

When she wasn't in Houston I would visit Suzy in Peoria whenever I could. I was divorced by this time, living with my son, Eric. He was just a little boy of four then and was confused as to why I was gone so much. I tried to explain that his Aunt Suzy was very sick and needed me with her. I felt better for having always told Eric the truth, but I know it was a difficult period for him. It was a difficult time for everyone who knew and loved Suzy.

The stress and tension put on a family involved in a serious illness is unimaginable. You know you must stick together on the crucial matters, so often the tension released is by arguing about the little things. My father had a terrible time. He could not bear the sight of his precious daughter being so ill. Like many men of his generation, it was not easy for Dad to express his feelings openly. It was impossible for him to accept the fact that in this case he was not the one in control. As a result, it was our dear mother who bore the brunt of much of the burden. At one point she stayed in Houston for five and a half weeks without ever seeing the outside of the hospital. She wouldn't have it any other way. Fortunately, Mom had the strength to go it alone.

It was especially difficult for her because during this time the lumps in my breasts kept reappearing. I had my left breast biopsied three different times during Suzy's ordeal. Once she had to leave Suzy's side in Houston in order to be with me in Dallas. All three of my tumors were benign (noncancerous). I hated to worry my mother, but the truth is, I was scared. Every time I felt the slightest little abnormality, my heart began to race. I had learned that women whose mothers or sisters have had breast cancer have as much as three times the usual risk of developing the disease.

Whenever we felt as if we couldn't go on, that the load was just too heavy, it was Suzy's grace and humor that got us through the day. She was able to find something to smile about with every turn of the road and her infectious, warm concern was felt throughout the hospital.

The one thing Suzy never found humor in, however, was the aesthetic conditions of the waiting rooms. The walls were empty, the chairs uncomfortable, and sometimes a patient would have to sit there waiting six or more hours for a scheduled appointment. Suzy was horrified and so was I. She was more concerned with the treatment of the patients while my concern was the treatment of the disease. I was outraged that more hadn't been learned to help my sister. "Nan," she said, "as soon as I get better, let's do something about this. You can find a way to speed up the research. I know you can. And I want to fix up this waiting room and make it pretty for the women who have to be here. This isn't right."

For about fifteen months the Houston team of Blumenschein, his associates, and Komen were successful in slowing down her breast cancer. But then, for reasons known only to God, the disease started to rage inside her once again. Fully aware of her condition, but never willing to give up or talk about it, Suzy began a perilous and painful downhill battle. There was more surgery and more chemotherapy, but by now her body had built up a resistance to the drugs. Her cancer had gotten so out of control that it broke through the skin, resulting in grotesque sores all over her chest. Her breast implant had to be replaced with some muscle from her back to restore the chest area. Plastic surgery after plastic surgery to cover up these lesions was performed. She also had an operation called an oophorectomy, which is the removal of the ovaries. In some cases an oophorectomy has been proven quite successful in slowing down the growth of the disease because certain types of breast cancer feed off female hormones. In some cases—but not Suzy's. She began to spend more time feeling awful and we spent more time feeling helpless. None of us knew what to do anymore. Up until this point we had always spoken enthusiastically about our future together. It was becoming more obvious with each new day that this *was* our future with Suzy.

I remember one afternoon at M.D. Anderson, we were walking from the hospital over to the hotel. Suzy had just been through an awful experience. Her lungs had started to fill with fluid and I watched as nearly a gallon of fluid was drained from them to keep her from drowning. It was very painful for her and I could barely stand to hear her gasping for breath. The street we had to cross was quite a busy one and as we waited for the light to change I saw a large bus barreling our way just about to pass where Suzy and I were standing. For a split second I contemplated the thought of how much easier it would be on her if she were to *accidentally fall* in front of that bus and end it all. I remembered her saying to me a long time ago that if she ever had to go through what Aunt Rose went through that she would want me to find a way to kill her. She'd rather be dead. I'm sure many of us have had similar thoughts, but when it actually happens the will to live becomes much stronger than anything else in the world. I wanted my sister with me for as long as possible *regardless* of the circumstances. *But the reality of the situation is that it really can get that bad.*

Another afternoon during the time when Suzy stayed in Houston, we were lying together by the pool at the hotel. She loved to sunbathe as often as possible, because she felt that having color on her face was the only thing that made her look healthy. As I watched her lying there reading, I took note of her thin, frail body and strained breathing. Fortunately, Suzy was *into* her book and paid no attention to me. Had she looked over, she would have seen my tears and known immediately what I was thinking. Our time together was drawing to a close. In a flood of beautiful memories I began to look back on the sacred relationship I shared with my sister. Frantically, I wrote my memories down, fearing somehow I might forget one later. I didn't realize then that memories so special are never forgotten. I also didn't realize that what I was writing that sunny afternoon was my sister's eulogy.

In quiet desperation, my parents, Stan, and I went to Suzy and Stan's rabbi for advice. He told us not to give up encouraging Suzy to keep trying but that under no circumstances were we to lie to her. It was time to begin saying our good-byes. Our family had always been totally honest with each other, and breaking that trust at this point would hurt Suzy much more than help her. Shortly after that discussion I was home in Peoria visiting one evening. My parents and Stan had taken Scott and Stephanie out to dinner and Suzy and I were home alone. She had just come back from Houston after an intense dose of chemo. I could hear her being violently ill in the bathroom. Throughout her three-year illness, Suzy was very brave and always maintained a great deal of pride in her appearance. I knew she preferred to be left alone at times like this. But on that particular night she just kept getting sicker and sicker and pretty soon I couldn't take it anymore. I ran into the bathroom and held her in my arms. "Oh, Nan," she sobbed, "isn't this awful? Don't I look horrible?"

"Yes, Suzy, it is horrible," I cried with her. "I can't imagine why this is happening to you."

After my sister was released from M.D. Anderson, I tried to come home every other week for a visit. Although she was too weak to get out of the car, Suzy insisted on riding with my parents to and from the airport when I came into town. Even though she could do little more than lie there in the back seat, this was her way of saying that she was still capable of taking care of me and that she was still there for me if I needed her. I did.

One particular Sunday afternoon on the way back to the airport, Suzy spoke to me again about doing something to help the sick women in the hospital. This practically tore my heart out because here she was, hardly able to manage a whisper, and she was worrying about other people. I couldn't bear it. When my father pulled up to the curb, I quickly kissed them both good-bye and jumped out of the car. I was just about inside the airport when I heard a funny sound that sounded like my name. I stopped in my tracks and turned around. There was Suzy, standing up outside the car on wobbly knees, wig slightly askew. With her arms outstretched, she said gently, "Good-bye, Nanny. I love you." I hugged her so hard I was afraid she might crumble. And then I ran to catch my plane.

I never saw my sister alive again. After nine operations, three courses of chemotherapy, and radiation, she had lost her three-year war. By the time I flew back to her side it was too late. She was gone.

Mother and I went to the funeral home to say a final farewell in private before her services began. When I approached Suzy, lying there so peacefully, I was shocked when I got close enough to see her face. My shock quickly changed to fury. Whoever had applied her makeup must have been the only person in Peoria who didn't know my sister. Her face looked overmadeup and phony, not at all like the soft, gentle woman we all loved so dearly. I insisted they remove all of the makeup from her face at once. And then, alone, with my own cosmetics, I reapplied her makeup the way she had taught me to do so many years before. Mom sat off to the side and just watched, while silent tears rolled down her cheeks.

The months after Suzy's funeral were the saddest in my life. I wanted to stay near my parents because I knew they needed me (the truth is, we needed each other), but I had a son and a home that had been without any attention for a long time. It was time to get on with it, to pick myself up and start living again. I owed that to Eric. Some things are easier said than done.

I spent a lot of time thinking about Suzy. There is no way to accurately describe the void her absence left in my life. I also spent a great deal of time questioning my faith and wondering why such a good person was taken from a family that needed her so desperately. I often wondered, as many people do when they've lost a loved one, what really happens to a soul when a person dies. Was Suzy watching me? Did she hear me when I called her name out loud? After much thought I came to the conclusion that I would never know until I died myself, but I sure as hell didn't want to die in order to find out. Just in case, I wanted to do something to let her know how special she would always be in my heart. I was haunted by our last conversation and lay awake sometimes all night wondering what I could do to help other women with breast cancer. *Could one person really make a difference?*

CHAPTER TWO

My Story

> . . . *love is the only thing that we can carry with us when we go, and it makes the end easy.*
>
> —*LOUISA MAY ALCOTT*

At a time when I needed a friend more than anything else in my life, in November of 1980, I met a man named Norman Brinker. Norman was and still is an extremely successful businessman in Dallas. I knew he was an eligible bachelor and had seen him at several charity functions in the city. What I had no way of knowing about was the depth of his character and the quality of his spirit. Norman isn't like any of the men I had previously met. He isn't at all interested in power. That's not to say he doesn't have any, he's enormously powerful. But he doesn't have to make other people look bad to make himself look good. Subjugation isn't Norman's style. He's a lover of people and a lover of life. I don't think he's ever met a person he didn't learn something from. He listens. There is a calmness about Norman that is a great balance for me.

From our first conversation, we knew we had a special bond. Norman had been married to tennis star Maureen (Little Mo) Connolly, and lost her to ovarian cancer in 1969. He, more than anyone else, understood my loss. We could talk about anything and everything, and we did. Norman taught me to laugh again, something for which I will never be able to thank him adequately. What seemed like a whirlwind courtship to most of our friends, seemed perfectly right to us. We had a great deal in common, including our love of horses, skiing, and politics. Norman and I married on Valentine's Day in 1981.

But for all my happiness and contentment as Norman's wife, I still wanted to do something about Suzy's dream. I wanted to fulfill the pledge we had made about the way women with breast cancer were treated and try to make the country more aware of its devastating statistics. I didn't have the faintest idea where to begin. Norman pointed out that I had had a great deal of fundraising experience for a number of different charities. He suggested that I put that energy into the cause that was now so dear to my heart. Of course—I would start a charitable fund for breast cancer research.

Breast cancer, I had learned the hard way, was the second leading killer of women in the United States. Yet, even in 1981, it was not easy to discuss the disease publicly. I was very sure that most of my friends had no idea that over 138,000 new cases of the disease were detected every year or that in 1940 one in twenty women were diagnosed with the disease but in 1981 the figure was one in thirteen. Throughout my sister's three-year illness, I had learned a lot about breast cancer, but I knew that if I expected people in Dallas to reach into their pockets, I'd better know a lot more about the disease scientifically. I studied with a vengeance. I called the National Cancer Institute and asked them to send me everything they could on the disease, and I read it. All of it. For a while, I'm sure I was an unwelcome guest at parties. I couldn't help myself. If a conversation started off about politics or childcare, I'd somehow manage to turn it around to mammography and mastectomy. I not only found the statistics of breast cancer horrifying, I was shocked at how little people knew or seemed to *want* to know about this enemy. The subject made people extremely squeamish, especially men. If it weren't such a serious matter, I would have been amused. They can talk about war with no problem. Murder is interesting. Bankruptcy is fascinating. But breast cancer? Next subject. I've always had the feeling that women's breasts were an easy topic of contemplation for men among themselves or in the bedroom, but discussing them with women in a dignified manner was a different story altogether.

Yes, I had my work cut out for me. It was clear that I had to gain the interest and support of women in order to get my project off the ground. It was also clear that this was an undertaking that could not be managed by one person. Together with a few friends who had, through personal experiences, a similar passion for the cause, I began my unending race for the cure of breast cancer. At this point, exactly what the "project" was, was still undefined. All we had were our hearts in the right places, $200 in cash, a borrowed typewriter, and a shoe box.

By the end of 1983, with a lot of hard work and a great deal of luck, we had turned that $200 into $150,000 (today the figure is over $9,000,000). Former First Lady Betty Ford had graciously joined our efforts and was actively involved in helping to make the country more aware of the disease. Because of her influence over my sister and the bravery and strength she exuded throughout her own battle with breast cancer, we established the Betty Ford Award in her honor. This award is given annually, by Mrs. Ford herself, to the person whose contribution in the area of breast cancer research or education is most significant. Additionally, we established several other monetary awards to nurture promising treatment break-throughs throughout the country. As our organization grew, we saw the need to establish an endowment to ensure our future, thus becoming the Susan G. Komen Breast Cancer Foundation. As our reputation grew, we began receiving requests for help from some of the most respected re-searchers in America. I cannot begin to explain the thrill of seeing our efforts make a difference.

One cold night in January 1984, Norman and I had just gotten into bed and I was pulling the comforter up over us in an attempt to get warm, when purely by accident and without any forewarning, as my hand skimmed lightly over my chest, I felt a small, hard lump in my left breast. I sprang out of bed screaming, "Oh my God, I have a lump!" Norman told me to calm down, to call M.D. Anderson in the morning and fly to Houston to have it checked out. If it hadn't been close to midnight, I would have gone right then. At the crack of dawn the next morning, I had Fred Ames on the phone. Fred is a surgeon at M.D. Anderson whom I had asked to monitor my breasts. I had become somewhat of a case study in Houston because of the family history as well as my own history of benign breast tumors. I had immense respect for Dr. Ames's work and a high regard for him personally. I told him this lump felt different from the others and that I was very concerned. He said for me to get on the next plane and come right down.

After feeling my breast and reviewing my mammogram, Dr. Ames said, "Nancy, I don't think it's anything to worry about. I really feel like it is another benign tumor. I hate for you to keep having this breast biopsied because it has been done three times already and you've got so much scar tissue now, it is going to be difficult to see what we've got in there. Let's watch it for just a little while and see if it changes."

Well, I took his advice and went back to Dallas. I knew Dr. Ames had good logical and medical reasoning behind his decision. But I had become an expert in the normal changes of my own breasts, and I knew *this lump felt different.* The other three had felt rubbery and this one was very hard.

The next day the Foundation was sponsoring a seminar on breast cancer detection. As you entered the room where the seminar was to take place, there were display tables set up with all kinds of written material for the guests to take with them. There were also several breast forms with hidden lumps in them so that the women could come by and feel exactly what we were talking about. As I stood there welcoming our guests, my hand fell behind me absently and I unconsciously began to feel the forms. Surprisingly enough, I had never done this before. I came across something that felt a little too familiar. One of the lumps in the form felt very much like the one in my own breast. As I stood in front of that group of women speaking about how important it is to be vigilant about your breast health, I wondered what they would say if they knew that at that very moment I thought I had a serious problem.

After the seminar I went to see my surgeon here in Dallas, Morris Fogelman. Dr. Fogelman had removed my previous three lumps and really knew my history. He was aware of the fact that I had since become a case study at M.D. Anderson, but I had always been very comfortable with him and just wanted another opinion. He said, "Nancy, that does not feel good to me and if I were you, I'd get it out." I didn't want to overreact and I had to take into consideration that Dr. Fogelman had said the same thing about my other three lumps, but I had a feeling he was right. He took me upstairs and did a test called transillumination (also known as diaphonography), which involves shining a bright light through the breast to illuminate its interior. Different types of tissues transmit and scatter the light in different ways. The test is read on an infrared-sensitive television camera. Studies indicate that transillumination, however, is unable to detect the tinier lumps routinely found in mammography. I felt the test was unnecessary for me. Although it was and still is effective in finding large lumps, I already knew I had a lump and wasn't looking for confirmation. What I wanted to know was whether or not I had cancer. Unfortunately, that can only be determined at this point by a biopsy or needle biopsy. Still, the radiologist who read the test said he, too, felt that my tumor was benign because it was a very round lump with clear definition all the way around it. The name cancer is derived from a Latin word meaning crab. When you picture a crab in your mind, its claws and legs reach out away from its body. The disease cancer is thought to do the same thing. It often spreads out in all directions, invading the healthy tissues and organs of the body. That is why having a perfectly round, clearly defined lump can be a good sign.

Once again, I went home and on about my business. There probably wasn't one waking fifteen-minute time span that I went without poking and feeling that lump. I swore to myself I could feel it growing. Ten days later

I went back to Dr. Fogelman. He said, "Nancy, it *is* getting bigger; get it out of there." Immediately, I called Fred Ames and told him I wanted this thing out—no matter what it was. He said, "No problem. Come on down—we'll do it here in the office. I feel very confident about it's being benign, but I know you're troubled so let's get rid of it. I'll give you a local anesthetic and do a biopsy right here in my office."

Norman was in Florida on business and my parents were also in Florida where they spend most of the winter. I called and told them I was going to Houston but that Dr. Ames felt sure there was nothing to worry about and that my friend Sandy would accompany me to the hospital. I made everyone feel I was not nervous, but the truth is I had a very uneasy feeling in the pit of my stomach.

Sandy and I were greeted at M.D. Anderson by Doris Bechtold, one of the patient-care coordinators at the hospital, a woman who had treated me and my family as her own from the first day we brought Suzy in the door. Dr. Ames brought me right into the day surgery room. I was given a local anesthetic so that I was completely awake and alert. A short curtain was placed directly under my chin so that I couldn't see the actual surgery, but I stared into Fred Ames's eyes for the entire operation searching for a clue. He didn't give me one. When a biopsy is done the suspicious tissue is mounted and sent to the pathology department for analysis. Some of the tissue is frozen and mounted on a slide for an immediate microscopic examination. Through the examination of the "frozen section," results can be determined in a matter of minutes. Analyzing the "permanent section" of the tissue can take several days. I wanted my results as quickly as possible, so I asked for both. I was wheeled into the recovery room where I waited for what seemed like an hour or more. All of a sudden, Dr. Ames burst through the door. I looked up at him and said, "Another false alarm, right?"

He said, "No, Nancy, it's not. It's cancer."

I remember leaping off the bed and screaming, "Tell me you're not telling me this! Tell me you're kidding! Please tell me what you're saying is not the truth!" And then I sobbed.

He walked over, hugged me, and said quietly, "Nancy, I sent it back twice because I didn't want to believe the diagnosis, but it is confirmed. You've got cancer. Now, I want you to calm down. It was very small and I think we've gotten it very early. You have a lot of options."

I just remember screaming, "I want them both off today. Get them off me! I want them off now!" I was so scared and so angry and so upset.

Fred told me to get dressed, call Norman and my mother, and then we would talk about the situation rationally. Well, I couldn't reach Norman, but I did reach my mother. She said that she would get Norman and they would both be there on the next flight. All I could think of was Suzy. I remembered how she didn't want a mastectomy and how desperately afraid I was of following in her footsteps. My mom asked me what I wanted to do and I told her to get rid of both breasts. Then I talked with Fred and he said he really didn't feel that was necessary. So, without another thought I said I wanted to get rid of the left breast for sure. As soon as possible. I was aware, even then, of a procedure called a lumpectomy, which only now has received the appropriate amount of attention and approval it deserves through fifteen years of exhaustive and brilliant study by a physician named Bernard Fisher. A lumpectomy is a surgical procedure in which only the cancerous tumor is removed. It is usually followed by radiation and sometimes other forms of *adjuvant therapy* (treatment other than surgery). When a lumpectomy is a clinically viable option, it saves a woman from losing her breast. Unfortunately, my tumor was located very close to the nipple, making it difficult to get to without totally disfiguring my breast. The cosmetic advantages of a lumpectomy, in my case, did not apply. I knew that if I could get through this alive, down the road I would have reconstructive surgery. To be honest, how I would end up looking was not a priority at the time. I simply didn't want to die.

I checked myself into the hospital right away and went through a whole battery of other tests. They did a full body X ray, a bone survey, and another chest X ray to see if the cancer had metastasized to other areas of my body. Doris Bechtold and Fred Ames never left my side. All the tests came out negative, but I couldn't allow myself to relax because I knew my lymph nodes hadn't been tested yet and wouldn't be until surgery the next day. George Blumenschein was away on a ski vacation. It would have been a comfort to have had him there.

By the time my mother and Norman arrived that evening, I was sedated, wailing, frightened, and confused. Both of them looked me in the eye and said they *knew* I'd be all right. I wanted to believe it and in a way I could see myself well again. Still, I couldn't afford to be too optimistic. Breast cancer is serious. The mental picture of Suzy at the end of her life, so small, shriveled, and weak, was haunting me. I was ready to fight and I wanted to get on with it. But that night I just wanted to be cuddled because the next day I was declaring war. Mother spent the night with me in the hospital. My breast burned from the biopsy, but I kept touching it anyway, thinking it would be the last time I'd be able to feel any sensation at all on that side of my chest. I thought about Eric and how frightened he must be. I thought about Norman and knew, although he'd never say, how frightened *he* must be after already having lived through the loss of one wife with cancer. And then I looked over at my mother, so brave and cheerful in the next bed. What must she be thinking? Was she preparing herself psychologically to lose another daughter after a long and gruesome illness? She seemed not to be. When she looked at me and said I would be fine, I searched her eyes for signs of untruth or pity. There were none.

The next thing I remember is being wheeled into the operating room the following morning. I touched my breast one more time before going under and then it was over. When I was wheeled back to my room, it was filled with people and flowers. I went to sleep feeling loved, calm, and content to be alive.

It must have been the anesthesia, because that contented feeling certainly didn't last. The next morning I woke up wanting to get going, to do whatever it was that had to be done in order to get well. Dr. Ames came to see me and said that although my nodes looked clear to him, the official results wouldn't be back for a couple of days. He also told me that he had made the incision in a place where reconstruction would be easy should I decide to have it down the road. I couldn't see anything at that point because my entire chest was bandaged down to my waist. With all those bandages I couldn't even tell that one of my breasts was missing. What I felt was a hot, burning sensation all over my chest. There were tubes protruding from the wrapping on my left side to allow the excess fluid to be drained from my body. It is the body's natural response to automatically send fluid to a vacant pocket of flesh. At first there is too much fluid to be reabsorbed naturally, so the tubes are usually left in place for approximately three or four days.

I wasn't in pain, I guess this is where the term *uncomfortable* comes in to play. Mostly I was restless. I wanted to *do* something. My family and friends were babying me, treating me like a sick person—and I didn't feel sick. The first moment I was alone, I got out of bed and took a walk through the hospital and upstairs to the physical therapy room. I knew exactly where it was because I had been there with Suzy. I got on a stationary bike and was able to pedal a couple of miles before one of my nurses found me and demanded I get back in bed. I looked around at the other patients exercising and thought how bored they all looked. There was a precious little boy in the room who couldn't have been more than three years old. My heart ached for this little boy. I looked at his lost little face and thought about how unfair it was that he couldn't be outdoors playing with other little boys. I thought about how Suzy would have reacted if she had seen him. It would have broken her heart.

Anyone who has had cancer or knows anyone who has had cancer or has even read anything about people with cancer will hear one thing over and over again: This is a disease that makes a person feel completely out of control. When you get a cold or the flu you can usually feel it coming on. You know the probable outcome and you can prepare for it if not avoid it. But cancer is something you can't prepare for. By the time you know you've got it, the disease has quietly invaded your body without warning. There are things I did in an effort to take control of my body which I am sure other people would not choose to do. Remember, I was a very well-educated cancer patient at the time and I had seen the disease at its worst. But nothing could have prepared me for the shock and fear of discovering breast cancer in my own body. I thought I understood it because I was so close to Suzy, but in truth, I didn't. Each case is special. It comes with its own set of specifics, both medical and emotional. All I was certain of was that I would do *anything* I could to rid myself of this breast cancer and get on with my life.

George Blumenschein was at my side within a couple of days following my surgery. He had spoken to Fred Ames, had seen my lab reports, and, as is typically Blumenschein, gave it to me straight—chapter and verse. He said, "Nancy, I think you are in a good situation. There was no node involvement and your tumor was still small. I feel very optimistic about your case, but I am going to recommend we treat this very aggressively for a number of reasons. First of all, your age. As a rule, the younger the patient, the more aggressive the cancer. Thirty-six is young to have breast cancer. And while your tumor was not wildly aggressive, it showed signs of being on the aggressive side, which can mean rapid growth. We also have to take into consideration the fact that your hormone receptor assay was negative [a hormone receptor assay is a test done at the time of biopsy to determine whether or not a breast cancer's growth is influenced by female hormones]. Today Tamoxifin may also be prescribed as adjuvant therapy. And your previous family history with the disease is very important. I want to bring you from an 85 percent survival rate to a 95 percent survival rate. And for that I recommend four courses of chemotherapy to begin as soon as possible, right after your surgery heals." He went on to explain that if I agreed to this form of treatment, I would lose all my hair and possibly experience other unpleasant side effects. Some people develop leukemia from chemotherapy; sometimes the hair doesn't grow back all the way. Some people get violently sick from the drugs, while others make it through the treatments with a minimal amount of discomfort.

Dr. Blumenschein assigned me to a protocol—a combination of drugs— being used in a clinical trial he was conducting at M.D. Anderson. I would be given several forms of chemotherapy including Adriamycin, 5-Fluorouacil (also known as 5-FU), and Cytoxan. In Part Two, Chapter 6, I will explain more about these and other forms of chemotherapy, but for now what is important to know is that this is a high dosage of drugs intended to kill off fast-growing cells aggressively. Dr. Blumenschein also explained to me that since Suzy's illness, improvements had been made in the subclavian catheter and pump. He said I could be very mobile if I chose this method of drug delivery and that there was a class available at M.D. Anderson where I could learn everything I needed to know about administering the drugs myself in the safest way possible. I did take the class and I did have the catheter surgically implanted. All I could think about was survival. According to Dr. Blumenschein, I could increase my chances of survival by 10 percent. That's all I needed to hear. I wanted to go home to Eric and Norman and give them the mother and wife they had counted on. At the time, nothing else mattered.

I am a lucky woman. I had the means to get the best medical treatment available. And I was educated enough to know how to find it. Still, there were those who didn't agree with the treatment I chose. Some highly respected members of the medical community thought perhaps the treat- ment I agreed to was *too* aggressive. Maybe I didn't need a modified radical mastectomy, a lumpectomy would have been equally as effective. Maybe I didn't need such a strong dosage of chemotherapy. What the outcome would have been with a less aggressive treatment, I will never know, but to those who think I should have handled it differently, all I can offer in a way of explanation is this: The informed decision was mine to make. I was fully aware of all my options. Between Fred Ames and George Blumenschein I had a medical team I believed in. I trusted their advice, but that's what it was, advice. I had to do what I felt was right for me. It was funny because when Suzy was so sick, I looked at her and thought to myself, *I could never go through this. I could never voluntarily choose to submit my body to such torture.* But when push came to shove and I was faced with the same life-threatening disease, the choices were not difficult.

Besides having money and education, I was lucky in other ways which proved to be equally as important. I had good friends and a lot of people depending on me to get better. I had built the Susan G. Komen Breast Cancer Foundation not only in the hope of one day finding a cure, but with the intention of helping women make informed decisions about their own breast health. I not only wanted to fight this disease, I *had* to fight this disease the best way I knew how. My reputation depended on it. This is not to say that I recommend my form of treatment to anyone else. Each woman has to decide for herself which options best serve her needs. She has to assemble her own team of medical experts and make her informed decisions based on their advice.

My team consisted of more than medical experts. I had a strong support team of emotional and spiritual members as well. I don't know what I would have done without my mother's help. She was with me every step of the way, and still is to this day. Norman convinced me that he would love me exactly the same with or without both breasts. I had friends who kept me laughing throughout the whole ordeal, which could have been, perhaps, the best medicine of all. One friend, Barbara Hyde, who was being treated for breast cancer at the same time as Suzy, made an especially touching gesture. She came in one day and discreetly placed something in the drawer by my bed. There were other friends in the room when she was leaving so she whispered softly in my ear that I would need what she left when it came time to leave the hospital. As soon as I was alone, I looked in the drawer and saw that she had given me a prosthesis. A prosthesis is a breast form, in this case a bra with one side filled with artificial substances that I wore after my mastectomy to look "normal" in my clothes. I was very touched by Barbara's thoughtfulness and appreciative of her sensitivity in not mentioning it in front of anyone else.

One afternoon shortly after my surgery, I found myself alone in the room quietly contemplating my future. The phone next to my bed rang and it was Betty Ford. She wanted to know how I was doing. Immediately I began to fight back the tears. The more she spoke, the more emotional I became. I was embarrassed and told her so. I will never forget her words. "Nancy," she said, "allow yourself the luxury of tears. Cry your heart out and say all those things you're feeling. Really pity yourself and ask, 'Why me?' You need to do all of that . . . but only for one day. Get it all out of your system and then release it. Let it go. You have studied this disease like no one else. You know what you have to do. Trust yourself and believe in your good judgment. Try to get through one day at a time. If one day seems too overwhelming, try to get through it one hour at a time. The rest is up to God, whatever 'God' means to you. There is a line from the twenty-third psalm that goes, 'Though I walk through the valley of the shadow of death . . .' Nancy, it says you *walk through it*, it doesn't say you have to stop there. You have a whole lot of people who love you very much and are pulling for you to recover." When I hung up the phone, I took Mrs. Ford's advice and cried my heart out. I cried for Suzy and for Eric and for my parents and for Norman. I cried for myself. The next day I checked out of the hospital.

It was time to start taking control. I didn't go straight home. My mother and I boarded a plane for California. With my chest wrapped in bandages and tubes still dangling, we headed for Los Angeles to purchase a wig. I had done some investigating and heard about a great wigmaker in Los Angeles. Supposedly, this man made wigs so natural-looking you couldn't tell them from the real thing. I have since learned it wasn't necessary to go so far away, but at the time I felt like I was positively acknowledging the inevitable and meeting the challenge head-on. I also knew that within my community, the word had spread like wildfire that I had cancer. I was already being called for radio and television interviews to discuss my disease and how I was planning to handle it. I thought the better I looked, the more positive the message I would be sending out. Immediately upon my return from L.A., I went to my own hairdresser and had him cut my hair very short. The wigs I had purchased were of short styles and I wanted the transition to look as smooth as possible.

This is something I had to do for me. It wasn't as if no one knew my hair was going to fall out. Of course, everyone I was close to knew what was happening. It was more a matter of preserving my dignity. I didn't want to give people any more reason to pity me. Letting myself go would have been, in my eyes, a form of surrendering to the disease. I was determined to stay on top of the situation as much as possible.

It was also very important to me to look good for Norman and Eric. Poor little Eric was so frightened. All he knew was that his Aunt Suzy had had breast cancer and she died. Now his mother had the same disease. He didn't understand the fact that mine was detected and treated much earlier than Suzy's or that my tumor was much smaller and not nearly as aggressive. At eight years old, none of that mattered to him. Norman was so sweet and kind and loving to me, but I didn't want him to think for one minute that just because Maureen had died, I would too. Her death was the most painful thing he had ever experienced and I wanted him to know that I was very much alive and intended to stay that way. She was taken from Norman just as his first chain of restaurants, Steak and Ale, was becoming successful. Now that his second chain of restaurants, Chili's, was enjoying the beginning of what would become enormous success, I sure didn't want to give my husband anything more to worry about. I also knew that my appearance was going to get worse before it got better. Remember, at this point, I was still all bandaged up, so he had yet to see his single-breasted wife. And although my hair had been cut very short, it was still *my* hair. No, the best thing I could do for the men in my life was convince them I felt well. That meant makeup, wigs when the time came, and the best general appearance I could possibly muster.

My mother volunteered to come back to M.D. Anderson for the four courses of chemotherapy. I felt awful to be putting her through the same hell she knew all too well, but she insisted. To be honest, I couldn't think of anyone else I'd rather have with me. I also knew what was ahead and it would be difficult to convince Norman I was well if he saw how sick the treatment was bound to make me. He had taught me to smile again, a few years back, and I wanted to make sure, now, that he kept smiling.

Like Suzy, I was not confined to the hospital. For the first part of the treatment I received a combination of 5-FU and Cytoxan delivered through an IV drip directly into the subclavian catheter. That was followed by four days of continuous infusion of Adriamycin through a small pump. I was given four vials of the drug to take with me over to the hospital hotel. As each of the vials emptied into the catheter a little signal went off to let me know it was time to make the change. It was kind of a tricky procedure because the catheter has to be meticulously cleaned in order to prevent infection. I am not mechanically inclined at all and really didn't enjoy fiddling with it. My mother was very helpful and made sure the job was done right. That night I felt pretty good, so Mom and I went out for dinner. I was in the mood for a thick, juicy hamburger and french fries, a treat I don't often allow myself. But I felt I deserved it so we threw our diets to the wind and really indulged. By the time we got to bed, I was content and tired, looking forward to a good night's sleep. It wasn't to be. At three o'clock in the morning I woke up violently ill, with the most wretched, flulike symptoms you could ever imagine. I was ill over and over and over again until I began to dehydrate, and Mother took me right back to the clinic. They gave me an IV and Seven-Up or Gatorade with chipped ice. And they put me on an antinausea drug.

Suzy used to complain of having a metallic taste in her mouth after chemotherapy and now I knew what she meant. I became acutely sensitive to all kinds of smells—things that had never bothered me before could make me turn absolutely green. It was a ghastly experience, but before long I had finished my first round and was home again in Dallas. They sent me home with all kinds of antidepressants, Valium and God knows what else, to try to relieve some of the side effects of the chemo. I tried to take as little medicine as possible. I've never been one to take a lot of pills, and I wanted to save the drugs for times when I really needed them because I know your body can build up an immunity toward certain medications. For the first few days I felt mildly flulike and then I started to feel good again. I got dressed every day and although I wasn't up for aerobics, I made it a personal goal to at least get out and walk even if it was just for a short time.

I was very self-conscious the first time I got into bed with Norman. I didn't quite know what to do or what he would think. I shouldn't have worried. He made me believe that it really didn't matter that my left breast was missing. I was much more sensitive on the subject than he was.

Nine days after my first round of chemotherapy I was sitting in front of the mirror brushing my hair and felt it happening. I looked at the brush and it was filled with my little short hairs. I cannot explain the feeling that came over me. Suzy had tried to describe it, but I didn't fully understand until I experienced it myself. A huge wave of panic took over my whole body. It didn't matter that I knew it was coming or that I was prepared for it. The truth is, I don't think you can ever be *really* prepared for going bald. That first day I was probably the only one who noticed any difference at all. I was terrified of what Eric would think. I didn't want him to be afraid of me. The next day, it was even worse—lots more hair in the brush. I felt completely out of control, the disease was gaining on me. I was there alone in my room crying, feeling terribly sorry for myself. Then I remembered Mrs. Ford's encouraging words and realized I had already done my crying. It was time to get on with it. I had to get back in control. I stood up, got into a steaming hot shower, and finished the job myself. I yanked every hair out of my head before it could fall out on its own. Then I sat in front of the mirror again and stared and stared at my head from all angles until I was comfortable with the new me, or at least as comfortable as I would ever get. I wanted to deal with the situation and face the facts. *As a side effect to getting rid of my breast cancer, I was going to be temporarily bald.*

I did my best to keep my round, bald head covered up at all times. I wore scarves and turbans, and my wigs. It was funny because that expensive wig I flew all the way to California to buy turned out to be more trouble than it was worth. In order for it to look absolutely natural, which it did, I needed a hairdresser to help me put it on. Well, I was anxious to get back to work and didn't have time for such frivolities so as a result, that expensive wig spent most of the time on the shelf while I wore inexpensive synthetic wigs I bought just around the corner. As time went on, I became more relaxed about the hair thing, though I never went to bed bareheaded. Besides the obvious reason of wanting to look as appealing as possible to Norman, it should be duly noted that a bald head is a cold head. You have no idea unless you've been through it how cold your body can get without hair. And, just for the record, your head isn't the only place you lose it. I felt I looked more like a plucked chicken than a woman. Eric did walk in my bedroom once and see my head before I could get covered up and I know he was really jolted. But that soon passed and before too long, he was back to acting like an eight-year-old boy. Sometimes when I was getting ready to leave the house, Eric would come over innocently to kiss me good-bye, and yank off my wig and run off with it. Naturally, I'd run after him screaming and soon we'd end up on the floor laughing until the tears streamed from our eyes. I was enormously grateful for those silly times because it proved that our relationship transcended the disease. I know I often took the anger I was feeling about being burdened with breast cancer out on Eric and Norman. It may have been a "normal" reaction, but it wasn't fair to them. They were, and are, so wonderful to me, I regret being robbed of even one moment of quality time together.

I went back to the Komen Foundation and resumed as many of my responsibilities as possible. As hard as I tried to look and feel good at home, I think I tried even harder at work. In my mind, I had to prove that I was the ideal cancer patient.

When April came, it was time for me to go back to Houston for Round Two. I had come up with another idea I was anxious to discuss with George Blumenschein. As much as I know the automatic pump is a remarkable device for many patients and that most people love it, I really didn't feel it was the best option for me. I realize that the pump allows patients their freedom to more or less continue with as normal a life as possible, but I am an impatient woman and wanted the whole thing over with yesterday. More important, I didn't like the idea of giving myself the medication. Quite frankly, I didn't really trust myself to do it right and I was tired of burdening my mother with the responsibility. What I wanted to do was check myself into M.D. Anderson and have Dr. Blumenschein put me to sleep, speed up the process of the delivery of the chemotherapy to two days, and be done with it. One night in the hospital, two days of treatment, and that's it. We discussed this idea at great length. That's one of the things I loved and still love about George Blumenschein—he always treated me with great respect and considered my opinions. We were truly partners in my treatment. He understood my reasons for wanting my medication in this manner and had come to know my impatience as well as anyone. He explained that I couldn't be knocked out completely during chemotherapy because if I got sick from the medication I could easily choke, and also that the process could only be speeded up so much. So we compromised. First, I turned in the pump I used for the initial course. I was allowed to be sedated but not asleep during the treatment. I did have four days' worth of chemo administered in two days' time through an IV drip. The catheter remained in my body for the IV, but I no longer had to fiddle with it except to keep the area clean and infection-free. The first time we tried this, it didn't go quite as smoothly as I had hoped. I still got pretty sick, but at least it was over a lot sooner. Today, thanks to a drug called Ondansetron, nausea is all but eliminated.

There was something about recuperating at home I found particularly comforting. Looking out of my own window at my own lawn gave me a feeling of inner peace. As I enjoyed the luxuries of home and family, my mind kept bringing me back to all the other women I had seen at M.D. Anderson who were not financially as fortunate. Breast cancer, like all deadly diseases, is expensive. What could the Foundation do for these women? It was then, in the spring of 1984, that the idea of a low-cost screening center was born. This idea turned into reality in 1986 at Parkland Hospital in Dallas.

I did notice something unusual happening after my second course of chemotherapy: I was having awful "black dreams." I have since learned they are a common side effect, but I found them horrifying. I could never remember exactly what went on in the dreams but they were dark, mysterious, and ugly. I would wake in the night absolutely terrified. In order to go back to sleep I would wander into the kitchen and pour myself a glass of wine, or two. It was the first and only time I ever thought I was drinking too much. It wasn't that I was drinking huge quantities of alcohol, but two glasses of wine every day on top of the pills and chemotherapy was taking its toll on my body. We now know that a person undergoing chemotherapy should stay away from alcohol altogether. It is not good for the system to mix cytotoxic drugs and alcohol. I felt lethargic and overweight and irritable. The realization scared me to death. I cut out the wine for a long time and focused on a healthy diet and a regular exercise routine. I began to feel better and noticed I was regaining my strength faster. Much to my parents' displeasure, I even considered starting to ride horses again. I began to set small, achievable physical goals for myself, gearing up to one big goal which was to play in a polo match by the end of July. Norman was worried too, but knew by now that once I had made up my mind he couldn't stop me. So he watched, and being a superb polo player himself, coached my riding and made sure I wasn't taking on too much too fast.

My third and fourth courses of chemotherapy went like clockwork. After a few minor adjustments in the combinations of the medicine, Dr. Blumenschein and I had found a way to make it work. It was, for me, a great accomplishment. The euphoria of completing chemotherapy was tempered, however, by a feeling of panic that I was no longer doing anything to fight the cancer. I was, of course, thrilled to be done with the treatment, but now what was I supposed to do? Sit back and do nothing? I couldn't help remembering when Suzy thought *she* was cured. Would that happen to me? It is a bevy of mixed emotions experienced by every cancer patient. The feeling is frightening, almost like the first day of school. You feel alone, timid, afraid to get back into the mainstream. I had been well taken care of by George Blumenschein, my family, and my friends, and now it was time to fly solo again.

The only thing that kept me sane was following the advice of another friend and cancer expert, the late Rose Kushner. She had said, "Nancy, always keep a full calendar. Don't give yourself a chance to worry and don't ever plan for a time when you might not be around to fulfill all the obligations you have made."

These were wise words, ones that I have repeated often to other cancer patients. This advice, in addition to striving for a physical goal, kept me going through that most difficult time period. I had set the physical goal, which was to play in a polo match by July. It was now time to prove to my friends that I was back.

I threw myself into fund-raising for the Komen Foundation. My friend Carolyn Williams had been working furiously to organize a function we called "Race for the Cure." It was an auction with prizes of a masculine nature, the purpose of which was to heighten awareness and support for breast cancer from the men in Dallas. It worked. *That night alone the Komen Foundation raised almost one million dollars for breast cancer research.*

I started to ride every day and had begun swinging the polo mallet once again. The truth is, it felt great. Yes, I wore out easily, but I also felt invigorated and alive. When it came time to play in that match, I was ready. I am sure I was a sight for sore eyes. It probably wasn't fair of me to

(4)Full speed ahead. The winter before my illness, 1983.

(5)Back in the saddle. With Norman
two years after my surgery (1986) and

(6) with Eric (1989).

54

put the other players through what they had to observe, but there I was, bald as a billiard ball, charging down the field with nothing under my helmet but a scarf. My mother and father were standing on the side of the field with a small oxygen tank, of all things, in case of an emergency. It was a blazing hot July day in Dallas and I guess they were afraid I would pass out from the heat. Norman and Eric were also there, watching on the sidelines. Our team won the match, and afterward, when the photographs were taken, I was the only player who didn't remove her helmet—a gesture I am sure was greatly appreciated by all. The victory, for me, had little to do with polo.

For the next year and a half I went through what my mother terms "the check-up crazies." My friend Carolyn Walker, also a former cancer patient, calls it "toe cancer." What it means is that every tiny ache or pain is immediately assumed to be the worst. You are torn between wanting to rush to the doctor every other minute and at the same time being scared to death to step into his office. Dr. Blumenschein had gone into private practice in Arlington, a city right outside of Dallas. I am sure I drove him nearly out of his mind, but he was always concerned, always ready and eager to see me.

It wasn't until almost two years after my initial surgery that I really started to look at myself and think about reconstruction. I was getting undressed for bed one night and happened to get a good look at my lopsided body in the mirror. I thought, "I really don't like this." My parents and Norman were going to be spending a great deal of time in Florida on business, and I just didn't want to be operated on or recuperating in Texas when the people I depended on most were going to be on the East coast. Although I am a knowledgeable cancer patient and like to think of myself as a strong woman, like anyone else, I want to be near people who make me feel safe when I'm not 100 percent well. My family does that for me.

After a lot of investigation, I went to a doctor by the name of John Bostwick in Atlanta, Georgia. Dr. Bostwick had published several textbooks on the subject and showed me dozens of pictures of his work. He told me how he thought the surgery should be done and how it would probably turn out. He also told me about the risks and everything that could possibly go wrong. I liked him and respected him right away.

The operation was fairly easy. Dr. Bostwick simply reopened the scar left in exactly the right place by Dr. Ames and slid in an implant underneath the skin and chest muscles. He did a little bit of mastoplexy (reduction) on the other breast so that they would match. Six months later I had the nipple put on. He took a little piece of skin from my thigh and fashioned the whole nipple areola complex so that it pretty much looked the same as the other one.

For the first procedure I was in the hospital for a few days. The surgery was on Monday, and the following Sunday I was watching Norm's polo match in Dallas. I was aware of the implant being there, but my whole chest area was still largely numb.

I was extremely pleased with the results and on the day I went to the department store to purchase my first *real* bra again in two years, I felt as giddy as a thirteen-year-old. It was fun to wear clothes that showed cleavage; I had almost forgotten what it was like.

The one problem I had not anticipated was lymphedema, which is swelling and collection of fluid in the arm on the side of the mastectomy. I knew all about it, of course, but had gone to great lengths to prevent it from happening to me. I maintained a low-salt diet, exercised the arm regularly, and kept it free of jewelry. I was very careful and therefore, not the lymphedema prototype. But about a year after my reconstruction, I accidentally burned my arm on the stove. It became infected and the infection caused my arm to blow up like a balloon. It was grotesque. I don't remember ever being so mad. Here I had suffered through the cancer, endured chemotherapy, worn a prosthesis for two years, and had a great success with my reconstruction. I had done everything possible to look normal again, and now this.

A breast surgeon in Dallas, Dr. George Peters, recommended a physical therapist, whom I saw every day. Some people told me that once an infection set in, the condition could be irreversible. George Blumenschein, too, had doubts about my recovery from lymphedema. But I wasn't going to accept it, not even from Blumenschein. As far as I was concerned, not making a complete recovery wasn't an option for me. I became even more emphatic about my diet, I exercised like a crazy person, wore an elastic sleeve on my arm all the time to try to bring the swelling down, and took antibiotics every day. Eventually, it worked, but the whole process took over a year. I am not sure that women are warned about lymphedema with enough urgency. It is a serious problem that, I feel, can disfigure a woman far more visibly than a mastectomy. To me, the mastectomy was easy to hide but when your entire arm, from the shoulder to the wrist, is three times the size of your other arm, now *that's* difficult to cover up. And, the *last* thing a woman needs to hear is that it is an irreversible condition. I didn't accept that, and I don't think any woman should. You know, sometimes patients can teach their doctors a thing or two about medicine. George Blumenschein often talks about what I taught him on the subject of lymphedema.

Although many have said it, it doesn't make the statement any less true: When you are told you have cancer, your life changes forever. *Forever.* I have always been a doer, always wanted to get things done yesterday. The long-term effect of having breast cancer for me has been to make me do everything in my life even faster.

I have no idea what tomorrow will bring so I don't wait for my future to run its course; I make it happen. I think it drives my family and friends crazy. Norman says I don't relax enough, that I push too hard. But I can't help it. There are a lot of things I want to get done while I'm healthy enough to do them. Subconsciously, perhaps I feel that if I slow down even for a short while, I am saying to those cancer cells, "Come and get me." Still, it doesn't do you any good to worry constantly about what *might* happen. That takes all the fun out of life. I have done everything I know that is possible to be healthy. I was beginning to have some very unpleasant female problems. The chemotherapy I received during treatment for breast cancer had altered my hormones and periods. My doctors felt that I needed estrogen regulation and that to give me estrogen would be inappropriate with my history of breast cancer—unless I had my ovaries removed. I decided to have a complete hysterectomy with oophorectomy. I am glad I did it. For me it was right. It may not be right for everyone. Some women do go on to have children after breast cancer, depending on the specifics of their disease. Given *my* family's history, I opted to forgo that possibility. The operation prevented me from having the one thing in life I might truly miss, a child with Norman. But we each have children, who together make our own family, which is more than some people *ever* have. For that I am thankful.

Now you know the whole story. I said I would tell you everything, and I have, at least all that has happened to date. Who knows what tomorrow will bring. At times throughout the last thirteen years, it has seemed to me and the members of my family as if we were acting out parts in some unfathomable novel rather than participating in real life. Other times we have felt so much a part of *real life* that the energy surges through our bones like a bolt of lightning. There is more to this, however, than the trauma experienced by my family. The good news is all that has happened

The Komen Foundation events are supported by many, many women and men, many of whom have undergone treatment for breast cancer.

(7)National Cancer Institute and Komen Foundation Summit on Mammography, Washington, D.C. Keynote speaker, First Lady Barbara Bush, 1989.

(8)Mother and the late Jill Ireland at the Komen Awards Luncheon, 1987.

(9)Former First Ladies Betty Ford, Nancy Reagan, and Lady Bird Johnson at the Komen Awards Luncheon, 1988.

(10)Former Vice President and Mrs. Quayle preparing for the Washington, D.C., Susan G. Komen "Race for the Cure," June 1990. The proceeds of these nationally held races benefit breast cancer research and development.

because of it. The thousands of women who make up the Susan G. Komen Breast Cancer Foundation have made enormous strides in bringing public awareness of breast cancer to the forefront. The money we have raised has helped to fund a number of significant research projects. For example, it has gone to the Johns Hopkins Oncology Center in Baltimore, Maryland, for the study of tumor growth factors; the Vincent T. Lombardi Cancer Research Center in Washington, D.C., for the study of tumor growth factors; the National Cancer Institute in Bethesda, Maryland, for the study of how the disease progresses in the body; the Peralta Cancer Research Institute in Oakland, California, for its effort to improve methods of early detection; the University of Texas Health Science Center in San Antonio for the study of drug resistance in breast cancer; the M.D. Anderson Cancer Center in Houston for its effort to analyze the genetics of breast cancer; the University of Texas Southwestern Medical Center in Dallas, where new immunology projects are being developed; and the University of Illinois, for creation of a research fellowship.

In 1987, the Foundation saw the need for a national network of researchers, breast cancer specialists, and treatment facilities and so formed The Susan G. Komen Alliance for the Research, Education, and Treatment of Breast Disease. The Alliance has three arms, consisting of the University of Texas Southwestern Medical Center, which will conduct research studies at the basic science and clinical levels to better understand the genesis, progression, and treatment of the disease; the Baylor University Medical Center, which concentrates on research and treatment of patients through two separate screening centers; and the Susan G. Komen Breast Cancer Foundation, which will continue its fund-raising efforts for national research, education, and screening programs. Every year there are new projects added to the list. We have also been successful in our attempt to change legislation in Texas so that insurance coverage for mammograms for women over the age of thirty-five is mandatory. We will not rest until similar laws are passed in all states. My great friend Max Fisher, Republican statesman and Jewish leader, says, "Politics is the art of the possible." I believe him. To help make screening and mammography more accessible, we actively support the development of screening centers in hospitals around the country. Currently there are six Susan G. Komen screening centers nationwide. Over 60,000 women are screened annually in Susan Komen–funded programs nationwide. Our Mobile Screening Van services communities where there are no permanent breast centers. Every day we do our best to reach new women, and enlist more fighters in this war. For information about screening services in your area, call (800) 4-CANCER or (800) I'M AWARE.

To this day, I am saddened by the untimely death of my sister. But I am with her every day through the Susan G. Komen Breast Cancer Foundation. The gift she gave me in life is one that I will cherish always, but the gift she gave me in death is the one for which I will be eternally grateful. It is also the gift she gives the world. If Suzy hadn't died of breast cancer, the Susan G. Komen Breast Cancer Foundation might never have been born. I would not have been inspired to learn the facts that saved my life or carry out her wish to educate other women.

Now, let's talk about you.

PART TWO:

You

CHAPTER THREE

Understanding Your Breasts

> *I'm just a person, trapped inside a woman's body.*
>
> —*ELAYNE BOOSLER*

*T*alking about breasts can be uncomfortable for a lot of people. Unless they are the subject of someone's joke, breasts don't usually come up in cocktail-party conversation. At least that is how it used to be. Our friends who have fought fearlessly to bring AIDS to the forefront of American minds have made breast cancer much easier to talk about in comparison. Breast cancer is not contagious, and that is probably why there is little feeling of urgency about the disease. Unlike AIDS, you can't get breast cancer from having sex. But it does threaten a woman's sexuality by virtue of its effect on her self-image. It also threatens her life.

A young girl's first sign that she is entering puberty usually comes when her breasts begin to develop. As she privately watches herself begin to grow, secret dreams of entering womanhood take shape. Developing breasts is a sure sign of more exciting things to come, though at that age she is still unclear as to what it all means. At first the impact her breasts will have on the young boys is far less important than the impact they will have on the other young girls. *Whose breasts are bigger? Who will get the first bra?*

Eventually, through schoolyard talk, motion pictures, television, and books, we start to become aware of the effect our breasts have on boys. As puberty turns into the teen-age years, we do what we can to make them look larger because we are taught to believe this makes us more appealing.

For Suzy, who grew up in the era when Marilyn Monroe was the big screen idol, having a curvaceous figure was very important. Tight sweaters were all the rage back then and she was very much aware that her good looks were credited to more than just a pretty face. Although there was only a three-year difference in our ages, Suzy and I were on the tail end of two entirely different eras as far as what style was in vogue when we entered our adult lives. While my sister and her friends were striving for a look of voluptuous femininity, my friends and I believed that "thin was in." Twiggy was our idol, and we strived for a look of slender elegance. For Suzy and me, the timing of the fashion trends was ideal. She was shorter than I am, about five feet, five inches, and although she was never over-weight, her figure was just like an hourglass. By the time I reached college, my height had caught up to my body weight and at almost six feet, I was tall and thin (the thin part was and continues to be a struggle). Our perceptions on what measurements constituted the perfect female figure were based on current fashion trends, peer input, and particular body types, and so differed dramatically. But, regardless of the differences, our individual self-images were extremely important and personal to us.

The importance of a woman's breasts to her total sexuality is embedded deeply in her mind at a very tender age. This happens long before a young girl can even begin to fathom the real physiological purpose of her breasts, which is, of course, to feed her babies. Although her maternal instincts are often nurtured in childhood through the use of dolls, those dolls come with a pretend bottle to complete the fantasy. Today, with the current trend toward natural childbirth and childcare, it is likely that a young girl will have the opportunity to watch her mother breast-feed a younger sib-ling. But, when Suzy and I were growing up, most children were bottle-fed; consequently, many women of our generation never fully understood that breasts were more than sexual objects. I know I didn't.

Even during the now commonplace *sex education* courses in the class-room, more time was spent on intercourse and pregnancy prevention than on breasts. Many teen-agers, although finding it fun to say they are taking sex education, are still embarrassed by the subject and are reluctant to ask questions in front of their peers.

The point is that it is not uncommon for a woman to enter adulthood having little more knowledge about her breasts than the best way to display them in a dress. In order for any of us to truly understand breast cancer, we must first understand the basic anatomy of the breasts, and how they function. Moreover, if we understand how our breasts function normally, we will be able to notice things that are not normal that may be signs of trouble. Too often, women wait until they feel pain before they go to their doctors. With breast cancer, this can be too late, for in its early stages it usually causes no pain. We need to take charge of our own health by understanding our bodies and not relying solely on our doctors to take care of us.

The Anatomy and Physiology of the Breasts

Each woman's breasts are unique in size, shape, and weight. The differences are based on several variables including heredity, total body weight, and the amount and type of physical exercise a woman gets regularly. Cosmetic plastic surgery must also be considered a variable today because of its growing popularity. Many women have breast enlargements to make them feel more feminine and attractive, while others try to improve their self-image by having breast reductions.

Breasts are glandular organs physiologically designed for one particular purpose: to produce milk. The structure of a woman's breasts changes dramatically throughout her lifetime, especially during the years between puberty and menopause. The normal cycle of female hormones affects both the outward appearance and the inside structure of the breasts, making visible changes almost daily. By understanding these normal changes as they occur, you will be better able to recognize any unusual changes that serve as warning signals for potential problems. But even if you *never* have a problem, it is important to know what is happening to your body. It is no longer acceptable for women to merely go along for the ride where their health is concerned. We have to drive the car. We have been content, in the past, to turn our bodies over to our doctors unconditionally as soon as *they* point out the first sign of trouble. Many people never see a doctor or a dentist unless they feel a pain. But this is a new era in health care. With routine check-ups, problems can be identified early when they are most easily treated. By knowing how our bodies are supposed to be functioning, we can use the medical profession to support our wellness rather than merely to treat our sickness.

It is crucial for a woman to understand the physiology of her breasts as well as their anatomical structure because of the close proximity of the breasts to other vital organs such as the heart, lungs, and liver. (Although a man's breasts are located in the same place, their mass, weight, and function do not have the same impact on the body.) The outward appearance of the breasts varies from woman to woman. Obviously the size of the breasts may vary but there are other common differences as well. Nipples may vary in color and appearance as may the areola. Some women may have small hairs and/or bumps around the areola, others may be smooth and clear. These differences are nothing to worry about.

If you could look underneath the skin and see how the breast is structured, it would look very much like the diagram on page 78. There are five major parts to the female breast: the lymph nodes, the fibrous tissue, the mammary glands and ductal system, the fat tissue, and the nipple and areola.

- *THE LYMPH NODES:* soft, bean-shaped structures which are the filtering devices of a microscopic network of tiny channels known as the lymphatic system that drain body tissue fluids and carry fluids that help the body fight infection. Fluids from the breasts are drained by two primary lymph node chains located under the arm and beneath the chest wall. These lymph nodes, referred to as the underarm or axillary lymph nodes, become quite important in breast cancer because they are one of the first regions to which the cancer can spread.

- *THE FIBROUS TISSUE:* extends from under the surface of the skin of the breast to the chest wall to provide support for the breast. It also separates the breast into segments. Younger women have much more fibrous tissue, allowing for firmer breasts.

- *THE MAMMARY GLANDS AND DUCTAL SYSTEM:* The mammary glands are the milk-producing glands. Milk is produced in the ten to twenty-five separate lobes of the glands during pregnancy and carried through ducts to the nipples during breast-feeding. The ductal system consists of the passages in the breast through which milk travels from the mammary glands to the nipple.

- *THE FAT TISSUE:* forms a covering for the breast. Its amount varies according to a woman's weight and age. After menopause, as the mammary glands begin to shrink, they are replaced by fat, causing the breasts to lose their firmness.

- *THE NIPPLE AND AREOLA:* The nipple sticks out from the breast. The ducts that carry milk from the mammary glands lead to the nipple, from which the milk is drawn by a nursing baby. The areola is the dark area of skin surrounding the nipple.

- *THE CHEST WALL:* consists of the ribs and a large group of muscles that fan out over them. These muscles and ribs form the firm background to which the breast is attached.

Normal Hormonal Changes in the Breasts

The breasts change in reaction to the fluctuation of the female hormones, both estrogen and progesterone, throughout a woman's lifetime. Some of the changes are day-to-day, the subtle enlargement and shrinkage of the breast as we near and end our menstrual cycle; some of them month-to-month, as in the pain that comes and goes monthly; and some year-to-year, the natural re-shaping of the breasts that comes with age, childbirth, and weight loss or gain. During puberty, estrogen production begins and affects the growth of the mammary glands. Fat in the breast increases and fibrous tissue becomes more elastic. Complete development of the breast occurs after ovulation begins with the effect of progesterone on the mammary glands. Just prior to menstruation the breasts are particularly tender.

During the menstrual cycle, changes in size and firmness take place because of changes in hormone balance. Breasts become larger and harder just before menstruation in preparation for a possible pregnancy. There is fluid retention and swelling of the duct glands. All areas of the breast are not affected to the same degree. Certain areas may be more tender or painful than others. As the cycle continues and pregnancy does not occur, the breasts readjust themselves. The swelling goes down and the tenderness subsides. When there is a pregnancy, the changes in the breast become more extreme due to the swelling and growth of the mammary glands and ducts. Breast-feeding maintains milk production in these glands.

During menopause, the breasts become smaller and softer because of the shrinking of mammary glands. At this time, the mammary glands are replaced with fat.

Becoming familiar and comfortable with these changes will help you to understand what your breasts are supposed to look and feel like on a normal basis. It will also become an invaluable piece of knowledge on which to base your concerns should you see or feel something that is *not* normal for you.

But how do you know what is or isn't normal for you? By examining your breasts routinely each month through a regular process known as breast self-examination. This process is described below. Your doctor should also chart what is normal for you by conducting annual physical exams and by mammography (X-ray examinations of the breasts).

Detecting Changes That Are Not Normal

The same three processes that indicate what is normal for your breasts—breast self-examination, an annual physical exam, and mammography—are also the best possible tools for finding problems in your breasts. Before discussing these tools, however, I should point out that not all breast abnormalities are cancerous. Hundreds of thousands of women experience breast lumps or other abnormalities at some time in their lives and never have cancer. So if an abnormality appears, you need not panic.

Breast Self-Exam

Breast self-examination (BSE) is one of the finest health habits a woman can acquire. Developing this habit is one way of taking charge of your body and becoming a responsible custodian of your own good health. A breast self-exam is an uncomplicated three-step process, requiring only a few minutes of your time each month. The best time to examine your breasts is seven to ten days after the start of your period, or for postmenopausal women, the same day each month.

The key to success of BSE is to practice the process religiously every single month. Remember, you will be looking and feeling for *changes* in your breasts. Skipping a month or two can make an enormous difference in the accuracy of the exam. After you have done BSE a few times, you will become familiar with the contour of your breasts and a problem, should one arise, will be something you can sense instinctively as well as feel.

The first part of BSE is visual, looking for changes you can see; the second and third parts are palpable, looking for changes you can feel with your fingers.

Step One: Performed standing naked from the waist up, in front of a mirror and in good light.

- Simply look at your breasts. They should appear symmetrical. Check for lumps, thickenings, dimples, or differences in skin color, all of which could be signs of a problem.

- Next, raise your arms above your head and look for the same irregularities.

- With your hands on your hips, bend forward slightly while tensing your chest muscles. This will make any irregularities more obvious.

- Check for nipple inversion.
- Finally squeeze each nipple very gently and check for discharge, another possible sign of a problem.

Step Two: Performed while bathing. Raise your right arm straight up behind your head. With your left hand soaped and fingers held flat together, press your right breast firmly against the chest wall and check for any lumps or thicknesses. Proceed in a set manner using one of the following methods:

- *(CIRCULAR)* Beginning at the outer edge, press the flat part of your fingers in small circles, moving the circles slowly around the entire breast and underarm area.
- *(VERTICAL STRIP)* Move your fingers up and down the breast in a line, beginning at the outer edge and working your way to the nipple. Don't forget to include the entire underarm area.
- *(WEDGE)* Divide your breast into imaginary wedges and move your fingers away from the nipple to the outer edge of the breast then back toward the nipple in each wedge. Be sure to cover the entire breast and underarm area.

Try each of these movements to see which one allows for the most sensitive feel. After you choose which one will work best, always use the same method each time you examine your breasts.

Repeat, raising your left arm and checking your left breast and underarm with your right hand.

Step Three: Performed lying down on your back.

- Place a pillow under your right shoulder and repeat the process you went through while bathing, examining your right breast with your left hand.
- Move the pillow under your left shoulder and examine your left breast with your right hand.

Once you become comfortable with this simple procedure, it should only take you about five or ten minutes each month. If you notice any irregularities or if anything seems even the slightest bit different to you from the previous month, do not hesitate to call your doctor right away. Don't worry about having a false alarm; it is always better to be safe than sorry.

If for any reason—physical or psychological—you have difficulty doing

*(11)*Breast self-exam. (COURTESY OF THE AMERICAN CANCER SOCIETY)

1

Before a mirror:

Inspect your breasts with arms at your sides. Next, raise your arms high overhead. Look for any changes in shape or contour of

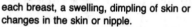

each breast, a swelling, dimpling of skin or changes in the skin or nipple.

Then, rest palms on hips and press down

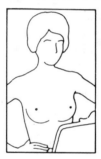

firmly to flex your chest muscles. Left and right breast will not exactly match — few women's breasts do.

Regular inspection shows what is normal for you and will give you confidence in your examination.

2

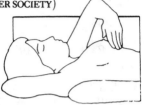

Lying down:

Lie down. Flatten your right breast by placing a pillow under your right shoulder. Fingers flat, use the sensitive pads of the middle three fingers on your left hand. Feel for lumps or changes using a rubbing motion. Press firmly enough to feel the different breast tissues. Completely feel all of the breast and chest area from your collarbone to the base of a properly fitted bra: and from your breast bone to the underarm. Allow enough time for a complete exam.

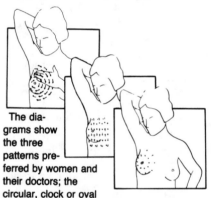

The dia-grams show the three patterns pre-ferred by women and their doctors; the circular, clock or oval pattern, the vertical strip, and the wedge. Choose the method easiest for you and use the same pattern to feel every part of the breast tissue.

After you have completely examined your right breast, then examine your left breast using the same method. Compare what you have felt in one breast with the other.

Finally, squeeze the nipple of each breast gently between the thumb and index finger. Any discharge, clear or bloody, should be reported to your doctor.

3

In the shower:

Examine your breasts during bath or shower; hands glide easier over wet skin. Fingers flat, move gently over every part of each breast. Check for any lump, hard knot or thickening.

WHAT YOU SHOULD DO IF YOU FIND A CHANGE

If you find a lump or dimple or discharge during BSE, it is important to see your doctor as soon as possible. Don't be frightened. Most breast lumps or changes are not cancer, but only your doctor can make the diagnosis.

WHY YOU SHOULD EXAMINE YOUR BREASTS MONTHLY

Most breast cancers are first discovered by women themselves. Since breast cancers found early and treated promptly have excellent chances for cure, learning how to examine your breasts properly can help save your life. Use the simple 3-step breast self-examination (BSE) procedure shown here.

FOR THE BEST TIME TO EXAMINE YOUR BREASTS:

Follow the same procedure once a month about a week after the start of your period, when breasts are usually not tender or swollen. After menopause, check breasts on the first day of each month. After hysterectomy, check your doctor or clinic for an appropriate time of the month. Doing BSE will give you monthly peace of mind. Every woman should have a regular checkup with a breast examination.

RISK FACTORS

- Being a woman over age 45
- Having a history of breast cancer in a close family relative (mother, sister, grandmother, aunt)
- Starting your period before age 12
- Having a late menopause after age 50
- Having no children or a child after the age of 30
- Being 40% or more overweight

a monthly breast self-examination, find a good nurse practitioner and have that person examine your breasts at least once every three months.

Clinical Breast Exam

In conjunction with your mammogram and breast self-exam, it is important to have a regular breast exam given by your doctor. A physician who has been trained in breast examination is sensitive to abnormalities you and I might miss on our own, especially if we have been negligent in performing our breast self-examinations. Many women have their breasts examined by their gynecologists, others by their family doctor. Ask your doctor if he or she gives the exam regularly. If the answer is no, ask to be referred to someone who is knowledgeable in the practice.

The exam will consist of essentially the same procedure described in BSE.

Mammography

Perhaps the best line of defense against breast cancer is mammography. A mammogram is an X ray of the breast. Many women resist having a mammogram because they fear exposure to radiation. When mammography was first developed, this fear may have had some substance because the dosage ranged from 6 to 8 rads per view, but today this fear is totally unfounded because new low-dose techniques have been developed that are not dangerous and do not cause cancer. Low-dose mammography is widely available now and can obtain fine-quality results while exposing women to a maximum of only ¼ rad per view, which is less than a dental X ray.

Low-dose mammography can detect tumors as small in size as a few grains of salt. Do you realize that the survival rate when tumors are discovered that small is 95 percent? For a tumor to be felt, or palpated, by even the most trained human hand, it would have to be at least the size of a pea. Many tumors are larger than this when first found, and most probably have been growing inside the body for several years or longer. When a cancerous tumor has been allowed to grow for that long, the chances are far greater that an aggressive cancer will have spread or metastasized outside the confines of the breast. The fact is that the survival rate for women whose breast cancer has been detected early by mammography is between 90 and 95 percent, while the survival rate for women whose cancer has been detected by palpation is much less, because cancers detected by mammography are often at a much earlier stage of their development.

Dr. G. W. Eklund, who heads the Komen Breast Center in Peoria, Illinois, explains the situation as clearly as anyone I've ever heard. "There are no known methods or devices to prevent breast cancer. The terrible realization that one of every nine women in the United States will develop breast cancer is made even worse by the reality that the incidence is increasing. The mortality rate remains the same as it has for decades [44,000 deaths annually]. In spite of it all, there is good news, even better news, and some of the best of all news. The good news is, there is a kind of breast cancer that is curable! The even better news is, almost all breast cancers are, at some stage in their development, this kind of curable cancer! The best of all news is, we have the ability to find these curable breast cancers! *Curable breast cancer is early cancer!*"

Knowing that mammography is the best way to detect early breast cancer, it is nothing less than horrifying to learn that still only 33 percent of all women over the age of fifty follow the recommendations for a yearly screening mammogram. Yet, most women over the age of eighteen *have* had a gynecological exam. Why do you suppose a woman would be so conscientious about the health of one part of her body and so negligent about the health of another? The answer is probably fear. Fear of hearing something she doesn't want to hear. Fear of losing a breast. Fear of abandonment by a loved one. And fear of losing her life.

But there is no need to be afraid. You should know that 80 percent of all breast abnormalities are not cancerous. Moreover, if the 20 percent of breast lumps that are cancerous are detected in their earliest stages, the likelihood of losing a breast is dramatically decreased. More important, the likelihood of death from breast cancer is also dramatically decreased.

Another reason women are reluctant to get a mammogram is the expense. It can cost anywhere from $30 to $200 for a good mammogram. The Komen Foundation and the National Cancer Institute together with other organizations have been successful in convincing legislatures in some states to change their laws so that screening mammography is covered by insurance for women thirty-five years of age and older. This has been a major advance in the war against breast cancer. It is important that you know and understand what exactly the laws are in your own state regarding mammography. But even if mammography is not covered by your insurance, think carefully about its value and the relatively low cost in comparison to your own good health and peace of mind.

Congress passed the Breast and Cervical Cancer Mortality Prevention Act in 1990. Through this act programs have been and continue to be

73

established offering breast and cervical education and screening with emphasis on the older, low-income, underinsured, and uninsured woman.

WHO SHOULD HAVE A MAMMOGRAM?

The National Cancer Institute, the American Cancer Society, and the Komen Foundation agree that every woman should have her baseline mammogram by age forty. (A baseline mammogram is simply your first mammogram, against which all your subsequent mammograms will be compared.) If you are at high risk (discussed in detail in Chapter 11) of having breast cancer, an annual screening mammogram is recommended after the age of thirty-five. A screening mammogram is an X ray taken to detect any hidden lumps. If you do not fall into the high-risk category, a mammogram every two years is recommended from age forty to fifty. Because two thirds of all breast cancers occur in women over fifty, yearly mammograms are recommended thereafter for screening purposes. If your doctor does not suggest a mammogram for you, suggest one for yourself. By now you understand the immeasurable importance of the mammogram and its value in your future. Be the custodian of your own good health. If at all possible, try to have your mammogram performed at the same medical office and/or by the same clinician each year to make the comparison easier. Your X rays should be safe in the facility where your mammogram is given. If you decide to change doctors and/or facilities, ask to have your X rays forwarded to the new doctor and/or location. These age recommendations do not mean you should not have a mammogram before age thirty-five. I am not going against what men and women far more educated in the field than I recommend when I say: *If you or your doctor feel anything abnormal, a diagnostic mammogram should be done immediately, regardless of age.* (A diagnostic mammogram is an X ray taken to confirm suspicions of an already palpable lump or some other abnormality which is causing either you or your doctor concern.) Remember that my sister's breast cancer was detected at the age of thirty-three, and she was dead at thirty-six.

WHAT IS INVOLVED IN A MAMMOGRAM?

The procedure is quite simple, takes only a few minutes, and is relatively painless. I say relatively painless because there can be a few minutes of slight discomfort involved. A typical mammogram consists of two views of each breast, top to bottom and side to side. In order to obtain the most accurate picture, the breast is pressed firmly between two plates. For women with especially sensitive breasts, this can feel a bit uncomfortable, though most women feel no discomfort whatsoever. Premenopausal women can minimize pain by having their mammogram done between five and seven days after their period ends. Think of it this way: It is less painful, has to be done a lot less often, and does you much more good than tweezing your eyebrows.

GUIDELINES FOR GETTING THE BEST POSSIBLE MAMMOGRAM FOR YOUR TIME AND MONEY

- First, go to a facility that does a minimum of fifteen to twenty mammograms daily. When a technician does not position the breast correctly, a lump may be hidden. If the facility does a lot of mammograms, it usually means the staff is proficient in the procedure. Breast centers, large hospitals, and special mammography mobile units are your best bet. Ask if the mammography unit has been accredited by the American College of Radiology or the American Osteopathic Board of Radiology.

- Make sure that the machine used to do your mammogram is "dedicated." A dedicated machine is used only for the purpose of mammography and not for other types of X rays.

- Find out who will be reading your X ray. The information can be given by the nurse when making your appointment. But ask the question again, of the radiologist, when you get to the facility. If the person reading your X ray is not an experienced radiologist (one who reads at least fifteen mammogram X rays every day), call or write the American College of Radiology (see Resources, page 189) for a teaching hospital in your area. Ask if the technician has had two months of documented formal training in reading mammograms. Does the person have evidence of formal examination in medical radiation physics, in radiation effects, and in radiation protection?

- Find out how much radiation is being emitted from the machine. It should not be more than 1 rad for all four pictures ($\frac{1}{4}$ rad for each picture). Ask if the equipment is calibrated regularly by a certified radiological physicist.

In summary, I cannot stress enough the importance of a mammogram. Detecting cancer early is your absolute best defense against advanced breast cancer.

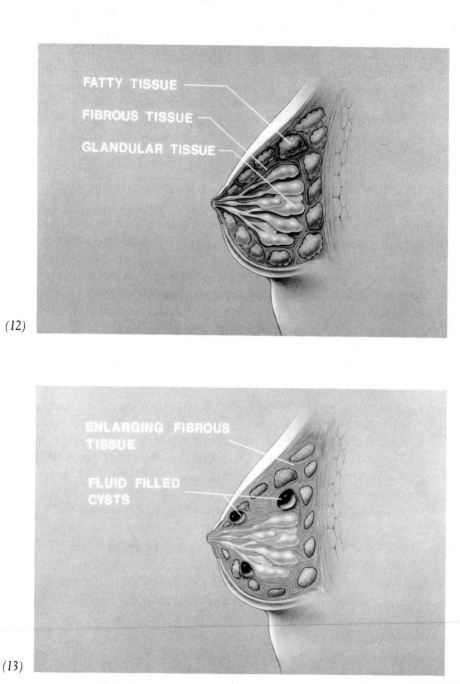

Benign breast disease. *(12)* Normal breast. *(13)* Fibrocystic breast, the most frequently occurring breast disorder. (ILLUSTRATIONS BY BILL MATTHEWS)

Benign Breast Disease

Noticing something abnormal in the breast will cause an intelligent woman some concern—it ought to. But as I pointed out earlier, it need not provoke immediate fright or panic. Eighty percent of all breast lumps are benign, which means noncancerous. There are many benign breast conditions that mimic cancer and can frighten many women unnecessarily. Brief descriptions of the most common of these conditions follow. Becoming knowledgeable about them should help you to understand more about your body and how it works, and make you feel more at ease if you notice anything unusual in your breasts. The important thing is to react immediately if you do notice anything. If you are even a little bit suspicious about anything at all, have it checked right away by a respected professional. Worrying is a waste of your time. The odds are that you don't have breast cancer, but if you do—waiting will only make it worse.

Please note: These descriptions must not be used to self-diagnose. If you have a lump of any sort, see your doctor.

Fibrocystic Breast Changes

This nonthreatening condition, in which multiple tiny cysts develop in one or, usually, both breasts, is by far the most frequently occurring breast disorder. It is often called lumpy or tender breast disease because the breasts may have an overall lumpy feel or distinct lumpy areas, which may be accompanied by tenderness or discomfort that fluctuates with the menstrual cycle, increasing just before the period begins. The condition, which is also referred to by doctors as mammary dysplasia or chronic cystic mastitis, is generally thought to be the breast's response to hormonal levels as they change from month to month over the years. Many types of treatments are recommended to alleviate these symptoms including mild analgesics, warm compresses or sleeping bras, a low-salt diet, restriction of caffeine (coffee, tea, colas, and chocolate), vitamin E supplements, and for the most severe cases, a special type of hormone treatment. Sometimes, individual cysts or distinct lumps may be felt. In this case, doctors usually perform a needle aspiration to evaluate the cause (see page 86 for a description of this procedure).

Now I need to say something *very* important. Please don't let the fact that both Suzy and I had fibrocystic disease *and* cancer frighten you unduly. This, as far as we know, was just a coincidence. If you have lumpy breasts, it does not mean you are more likely to develop cancer. It does mean that you need to be especially aware of the normal changes your breasts go through regularly so that your hand and eye are alert to changes that may be abnormal. With that in mind, remember that *nearly all women's breasts develop some degree of lumpiness.*

Fibroadenoma

Fibroadenoma is a solid benign tumor composed of fibrous and glandular tissue. It is painless and movable and has a rubbery feel. Usually it occurs singly, but it can occur multiply and be found in both breasts. Although this tumor is most frequently found in women aged twenty to forty, fibroadenomas are the most common mass found in girls prior to puberty.

Cysts

Cysts are fluid-filled sacs. In the breast, they can be small enough to go unnoticed by the hand and eye or large enough to hold as much as a quarter cup of fluid. You could have one or two isolated cysts, or fibrocystic disease, which is recurring cysts.

Ductal Papillomas

Ductal papillomas are small, benign finger-like growths in the mammary ducts close to the nipple. The growths, which are usually difficult to feel, cause a bloody discharge from the nipple. This condition occurs most often in, but is not limited to, women between the ages of forty-five and fifty.

Mammary Duct Ectasia

This is a condition unique to women near or past menopause, wherein the ducts in or beneath the nipples become clogged with fat, producing a lump. Symptoms are burning and itching around the nipple or occasionally a dark discharge from the nipple.

Fat Necrosis

Fat necrosis, the death of tissue following an injury or surgery to the breast, usually results in a painful lump. This condition can occur at any age.

Galactocele

This is a clogged milk duct associated with child birth that can affect both breast-feeding and non-breast-feeding mothers.

In Summary

Although an abnormality in your breasts does not necessarily mean cancer, this does not mean you can put off consulting your doctor about it. It is important to have a diagnosis made as soon as possible so that if it should be cancer, you can catch it before it has a chance to spread.

In the next chapter I describe what should be done if an abnormality appears, and how a diagnosis is made.

CHAPTER FOUR

Understanding Breast Cancer and How It Is Diagnosed

*Life is something
that happens to you
while you're
making other
plans.*

—MARGARET
MILLAR

If an abnormality should appear in one of your breasts, you will need to discover as soon as possible whether it is a benign breast disease or cancer. In order to understand what needs to be done, it is important that you know something about breast cancer itself.

Understanding breast cancer won't enable you to escape the disease, but it could save your life. It saved mine. At present there is nothing we can do to prevent breast cancer. There is some work being done to show how a low-fat diet may be beneficial. But if we catch it in its earliest stage, optimally we can expect a 95 percent chance of survival. To me, that makes it worth learning about.

What Is Breast Cancer?

Some people call it "the C Word," others refer to it as "the Big C," still others won't refer to it at all. The truth is, no one likes to talk about cancer. And because no one likes to talk about it, many people don't even know what it is, other than a disease that can kill you. I will try to define it here in simple terms.

Healthy cells that make up the body's tissue grow, divide, and replace themselves in an orderly manner. Sometimes cells lose their ability to control their growth. They divide too rapidly and grow out of control, forming masses or tumors. These tumors, which can expand by invading and destroying healthy tissues and organs, are cancer. Cancerous tumors are called malignant because they are potentially fatal. Tumors can also arise in the body that do not spread by invasion and are therefore not usually life-threatening. These noncancerous tumors are referred to as benign. (An example of a benign tumor is the fibroadenoma, discussed on page 80.) A malignant tumor is very dangerous because it can invade healthy tissues and organs not only locally (adjacent to itself) but also in other parts of the body, to which it travels through the bloodstream and the lymphatic system. This systemic spreading, known as metastasis, usually does not occur until the cancer has grown for a period of time.

Some breast cancers remain confined to either the duct or lobule (in situ cancer), while others grow into the surrounding tissue (invasive or infiltrating). The most common type of breast cancer is infiltrating ductal carcinoma. Breast cancer can spread regionally to the underarm or axillary lymph nodes. Spread to distant body areas is referred to as metastasis. The most common areas for metastasis are the lungs, bones, liver, and brain.

Signs of Breast Cancer

When breast cancer begins, it rarely causes pain or other obvious symptoms that might alert you that something is wrong. But as a cancerous growth develops, it may take on several different outward appearances that act as warning signs.

- *A LUMP:* most often felt and not seen by the human eye in its early stages. It is usually single, hard, and painless.
- *INVERTED NIPPLE:* Every once in a while, a nipple will be naturally inverted. But if you notice your nipple becoming inverted after previously being normal, this could be a sign of danger.
- *SKIN SWELLING:* when a portion of the skin becomes bumpy, much like the appearance of an orange peel.
- *SUPERFICIAL VEINS:* when the veins closest to the skin become obviously more prominent on one breast than the other.
- *SKIN DIMPLING:* when a depression occurs in a particular area of the breast surface.

These are the most obvious warning signals for breast cancer. However, it cannot be stressed enough that if you notice anything at all out of the ordinary, you should report it to your doctor immediately.

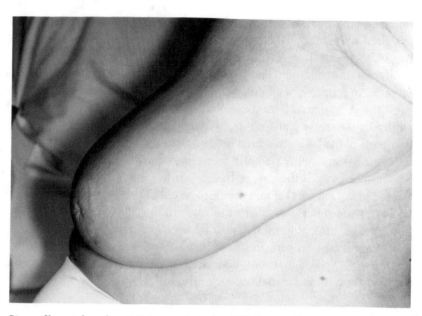

(14)

Signs of breast disorder. *(14)* Inverted nipple. *(15)* Skin swelling. Note the bumpy area around the nipple. *(16)* Inflammatory carcinoma, characterized by a rash-like area. (PHOTOS COURTESY OF DR. GEORGE PETERS)

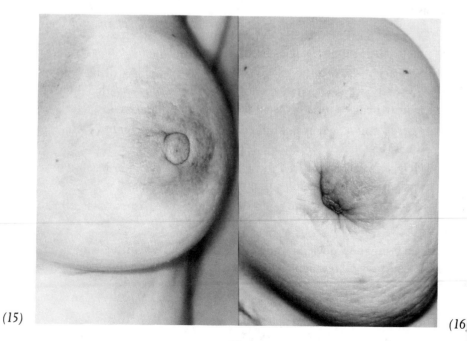

(15)

(16

If an Abnormality Appears

Let's go over exactly what should be done, step by step, in the event of even the most minute abnormality. I like to use plain language, for I know how intimidating medical terminology can be. If you thoroughly understand it now, you will be better able to recall the information at the time when you need it most. Keep in mind that no two cases of breast cancer are exactly the same. Diagnosis and treatment procedures must be individualized according to many factors unique to the woman involved. However, it is useful to understand what the various possibilities are so that, if nothing else, you have a starting point on which to base your own questions.

The First Step: Finding the Right Doctor

If you have a lump in your breast, chances are that it was detected one of four ways: (1) You found it yourself through BSE or by accident (which was the way I found my own cancer); (2) it was noticed by a sexual partner and brought to your attention; (3) it was discovered by your doctor during a medical exam; or (4) it showed up during a screening mammogram. If the lump was detected by options 3 or 4, your advantage is that at least you are under a doctor's supervision. You have a place to begin, someone to whom you can direct your questions. But if you found the lump yourself or if it was found by a sexual partner, where do you go first? Whom do you call?

Women in the United States most often turn to their gynecologists when they have any kind of personal physical problem. For this reason, many GYNs have made it a point to become knowledgeable about breast diseases. Whether you choose to see your gynecologist, a general practitioner, or any other family doctor you feel comfortable with, don't hesitate for a moment to ask if he or she has a special interest in the detection and diagnosis of breast disease. If the answer is no, ask to be referred to a breast specialist. Even if the answer is yes, you may want to see a breast specialist for evaluation, confirmation, and additional tests if they become necessary.

You should be aware that a breast specialist is a rather rare commodity. "It is sad," admits Dr. G. W. Eklund, head of the Komen Breast Center in Peoria, Illinois, "that so many physicians providing primary care for women openly admit their omission of a breast examination as part of the routine physical, or frankly admit that they feel poorly equipped to evaluate and treat breast disorders, benign or malignant. Considering the magnitude of breast-related diseases, it is curious if not tragic that 'mastology' has not emerged as a major field of practice. We are just beginning to see a few surgeons taking an additional fellowship year in breast surgery and limiting their practice to diseases of the breast. A few radiologists are doing the same thing with regard to diagnostic imaging of the breast."

But what if you are without a doctor at all? Perhaps you are new to an area or on vacation. Usually everyone has access to a nearby hospital that can refer them to a specialist. In the event you are in an extremely rural part of the country or are not comfortable with the physician you know, there are several organizations listed in the Resources section of this book that can help you find a good doctor as nearby as possible. In particular, see the National Cancer Institute (page 191), the American Cancer Society (page 189), the "Y-ME" hotline in some states and the Susan G. Komen Breast Cancer Foundation (page 192), which all have toll-free phone numbers. Remember that you are not alone. There are people to help you get through this and come out with a treatment plan.

Diagnostic Testing

Once a lump is detected and you are in the care of a doctor you trust, there are several important diagnostic steps that can follow. First, if you haven't had a *mammogram*, you will. This will give both you and your doctor a clearer picture of the specific location of the lump and its exact size.

It is possible your lump may be nothing more than a fluid-filled cyst. If this is the case, it can be determined immediately, in the doctor's office by a *"needle aspiration."* Using a needle and syringe, your doctor will attempt to extract fluid from the lump. If you have a cyst, the syringe will fill up with fluid and the wall of the cyst will collapse, much like what would happen if you poked a needle into a balloon filled with water.

If the lump is solid, nothing will be obtained by aspiration and a *biopsy* will be in order. A biopsy may also be in order if the fluid extracted from the cyst is bloody or looks suspicious in any way. Biopsy, the removal and microscopic examination of tissue to see if cancer cells are present, is discussed on page 87.

There are other tests that may be suggested to get a different perspective on the suspicious mass before a biopsy is performed. It is important that you know what they are and their purpose in order to make the experience less frightening. Remember that none of these tests has been proven effective enough to replace mammography screening. They must be used in conjunction with your mammogram or not at all. A mammogram can more clearly define whether a mass or lump has clear margins—that is, clear edges.

- *XEROMAMMOGRAPHY:* a form of mammography in which the films are printed on paper and do not require an X-ray view box to be evaluated.

- *ULTRASONOGRAPHY:* uses sound waves to produce echoes which can be photographed and viewed on a screen. These sound waves can distinguish the presence of an abnormal tissue and can separate solid from cystic masses. Studies have proven, however, that ultrasonography can miss a significant number of nonpalpable tumors that can be easily identified with mammography.

- *DIAPHANOGRAPHY:* a technique in which a bright light is shown through the breast onto an infrared-sensitive screen. Tumors, if present, will appear as a dark mass. This technique, also called transillumination, has proven in research studies to miss the smaller masses and is not very reliable.

- *THERMOGRAPHY:* measures and records heat patterns in the breast. This test is based on the principle that the blood flow to tumors is warmer than the blood flow to normal tissues. This procedure has tested as highly inaccurate in detecting small cancers and is not often recommended.

- *MAGNETIC RESONANCE IMAGING (MRI):* a new, experimental technique that uses the interaction between magnetism and radiowaves to picture the structure of biological tissues. Once again, this technique has proven successful in imaging large, palpable tumors, but it is unclear how well MRI can distinguish between benign and malignant breast tumors. This procedure is still being tested.

- *COMPUTERIZED AXIAL TOMOGRAPHY (CAT OR CT) SCANNING:* still in the experimental stage. Using X rays, the scanner rotates around the patient, taking pictures from all angles. The information is then reproduced on a video screen. The one advantage proven thus far is that computerized tomography, or CAT, scanning can be useful in detecting tumors in small, dense breasts that are sometimes difficult to detect in mammography.

Biopsy

Effective as it is in detecting early tumors, mammography has not eliminated the need for surgical biopsy when trying to decipher whether or not a breast mass is benign or malignant. There are four types of biopsy procedures, two of which are surgical.

- *FINE-NEEDLE ASPIRATION:* performed in the doctor's office. A fine needle is inserted into the suspicious mass and cells are sucked out, placed on a glass slide, and studied under a microscope.

- *CORE NEEDLE BIOPSY:* also performed in the doctor's office; uses a special kind of needle that removes a plug of tissue, which is then examined and studied under a microscope.

- *THE INCISIONAL BIOPSY:* a surgical procedure in which part of the suspicious mass is removed; performed in the hospital or in day surgery under either local or general anesthesia. This procedure is rarely done anymore because studies have shown that a tumor may consist of both benign and malignant cells, so removing only part of the tumor could result in a false negative report from the pathologist. (A pathologist is a doctor who specializes in the diagnosis of disease by studying the cells and tissues removed from the body.)

- *EXCISIONAL BIOPSY:* a surgical procedure in which the entire lump is removed; also done in the hospital or in day surgery under either local or general anesthesia. Since the entire mass is removed, it is preferable to the incisional procedure.

If fine-needle aspiration or core needle biopsy fails to provide a definite diagnosis, then you will need a surgical biopsy, most likely an excisional biopsy. There is an important decision to be made before your surgical biopsy is done, which requires serious and honest communication between you, your doctor, and perhaps with one or more loved ones. Generally the biopsy and any definitive surgery for breast cancer are separated by a space of time ranging anywhere from several days to 2 or 3 weeks. The important issue is that women do not have to go under anesthesia wondering if they will awake with or without their breast. Although the tendency is to act quickly and get it—the cancer—out, there is usually not any medical necessity to do so. Women need time to get as much information as possible in order to make an informed decision about treatment choices. Get a second opinion. If breast conservation is offered, see not only the surgeon, but the radiation oncologist. Talk with a medical oncologist.

The biopsy and surgery are most often scheduled as separate steps. Recent studies have proven that a *short* delay between biopsy and treatment will not affect the spread of the disease or decrease the chance of successful treatment. If you opt for the two-step procedure, you will probably go into the hospital on an outpatient basis but may be required to stay overnight, depending on the biopsy itself, how you are feeling, and the scheduling of the surgery. The same laboratory tests will have to be done as discussed in the one-step procedure prior to surgery. Some women prefer to have the lab tests done several days before their biopsy; other women find it easier to get everything taken care of in one visit to the hospital. If you are scheduled for outpatient surgery, the tests will most likely have to be done beforehand. You can receive either local or general anesthesia during the biopsy and leave the hospital within hours of your surgery.

After the biopsy is completed, both the frozen section and the permanent section are analyzed for cancer cells. You will have confirmed results within a couple of days. As is always the case, the waiting can be torture. But the advantages of the two-step procedure can, for some women, be significant. Should your tumor be cancerous, the short delay (not more than two weeks) in treatment provides you with the opportunity to prepare yourself for what comes next—emotionally, medically, and intellectually— and to seek other opinions.

Other Tests Done at the Time of Biopsy

There are a number of other tests that will be performed on the tissue that is removed in biopsy. Before your biopsy, you and your doctor should discuss each test he or she intends to perform and why. It is important that you understand everything that is being done to you so that you can become a partner in your treatment.

Hormone Receptor Assay

It is important that hormone receptor assays (tests) are done at the time of your biopsy if a malignancy is found. The hormone receptor assay—one for estrogen and one for progesterone—will determine whether or not your cancer is hormone-dependent, and whether hormonal therapy will benefit you now or later in your treatment. (Hormonal therapy is discussed in Chapter 6.) This assay will give the physician very important clues about which adjuvant treatment may be more effective. Estrogen positive or estrogen rich tumors tend to respond better to hormone drugs. Estrogen negative tumors tend to be treated with chemotherapy. About 75 to 80 percent of postmenopausal women have estrogen positive tumors while only 25 to 30 percent of premenopausal women have estrogen positive tumors. Whether you are pre- or postmenopausal and whether the tumor is estrogen negative or positive impact the treatment decision markedly. Any woman undergoing a breast biopsy should insist that these tests are done immediately following cancer detection. And be aware that it may take as long as seven to ten days to get the results of these tests back from the laboratory.

FLOW CYTOMETRY

Another test commonly done today on cancerous tissue at the time of biopsy is called flow cytometry, which shows the aggressiveness of the tumor. Flow cytometry yields two results: whether the cancer has extra chromosomes (aneuploidy) and how fast it is growing (S-phase). Knowing how fast your cancer is growing is an important factor in determining your treatment options.

CATHEPSIN D

This assay must be performed at the time of the biopsy. Cathepsin D is an enzyme that is secreted by normal cells but is produced in greater amounts by breast cancer cells. High levels of this enzyme increase the risk for recurrence. Once the test becomes more conclusive it may prove to be a very important prognostic indicator.

ONCOGENE TESTING

An oncogene is a genetic defect that causes the cell to go haywire and to multiply at an abnormal speed to produce other abnormal cells. In other words, the oncogene initiates the very first cancerous cell of any cancer that develops. Doctors hope that by developing tests that will reveal the presence of the oncogene in the body, they can take measures to block its effects. The hope is that cancer will be something that can be stopped before it begins. Much research is being done in this area. Soon, physicians will be able to use an assortment of these predictive means to be able to more accurately diagnose a breast cancer, predict recurrence, and prescribe the best treatment.

CHAPTER FIVE

Choosing a Support Team

> *You have to accept whatever comes and the only important thing is that you meet it with courage and the best you have to give.*
>
> —*ELEANOR ROOSEVELT*

If you are diagnosed as having breast cancer, the first thing you must do is try to stay calm. I realize that may seem like a silly thing to say. I didn't stay calm and I was a highly educated cancer patient. But remember this: *Being diagnosed with breast cancer does not mean you have been handed a death sentence.* What it does mean is that you have a serious problem for which you have many options. In the next several chapters I am going to try to guide you through this, as a friend and as a cancer survivor. I am not a doctor; I wouldn't presume to give medical advice. What I can do for you, what I want to do for you, is to discuss the disease openly and honestly so that you have a basis for actively participating in the decisions about which options are best for you.

I have found that we, as women, have a tendency to give ourselves up to doctors unconditionally. Dr. Wendy Schain, Director of Adult Psychological Oncology at the Memorial Cancer Institute, Long Beach, California, puts it this way: "There is something about seeing the two initials M.D. after a name that allows us to give up our right to question their [our doctor's] authority." We must get over this. We owe it to ourselves to ask as many questions as necessary to fully understand our situation.

When you first receive your diagnosis of breast cancer, you will probably be overwhelmed with conflicting emotions.

If there was ever a time for a little self-indulgence, it's now. As Betty Rollin so eloquently put it in her book, *First, You Cry,* you need to allow yourself to release the emotion you feel after being told you have a life-threatening disease. Cry, scream, get mad, feel sorry for yourself—do all of these things if you want. Not only do you deserve it, but expressing yourself honestly will help relieve the stress. But as Betty Ford suggested to me, try to limit the hysteria to a day or two, and then put it behind you. Carrying on indefinitely will affect your ability to take an effective part in the decision-making process now ahead.

It is natural to feel resentful and afraid, victimized and confused. But you need not feel helpless, because there is always something that can be done in an attempt to save or prolong your life. It is your family and those who love you who will feel helpless. You can help them by taking care of yourself.

The best way to take care of yourself I know is to learn as much as you can about what your options are and then decide for yourself which ones best serve your needs—psychologically and practically, as well as medically. To do that you need to assemble a team of experts you trust to give you medical advice and emotional support. Then, ask questions, and keep asking until you understand and are satisfied with the answers. You then will be prepared to embark upon the informed decision-making process that will establish your treatment strategy.

With the help of your team of experts, you can take control of the situation. But remember, the final decisions should be yours.

My Own Support Team

My mother always told me to remember my sense of humor, even in the most difficult situations because those are the times when it is needed most. Whenever I meet a new doctor, whether it is for my own personal health or for the Foundation, I can't help but think of Erma Bombeck's funny quote, "Never go to a doctor whose office plants have died."

When cancer was detected in my left breast nine years ago, I affectionately referred to the group of people I depended on most during that crucial time period as my A Team. But the truth is, this group of individuals was and continues to be a guiding force in my life. None of the people on my team were there by accident. I strategized and thought about each one of them and they all have their own individual roles in my continued recovery.

The A had a double meaning to me: First, it stood for excellence—representing the best possible group of individuals for my own personal needs; and second, it stood for *attack*. After I got control of my emotions, I was determined to attack my cancer with everything I had.

My advantage over some of you is that my team was pretty much in place *before* my cancer was diagnosed. After living through my sister's illness, going through three previous biopsies, and establishing the Komen Foundation, I already knew which individuals would give me the best possible support I needed, both medically and emotionally. I will share with you how and why the members of my team were chosen, though your needs may be completely different. As in all avenues of cancer treatment, what is right for one person is not necessarily right for another. Every case is different, every woman is an individual. But hearing the way I thought about it may give you a start, if nothing else, in choosing your own A Team. I believe every cancer patient should have one.

The Medical Members

Before I tell you about the medical members of my team, I should mention the various different doctors you will need, and why. The best possible team would be: a surgeon, an oncologist, a pathologist, a radiologist, and a plastic surgeon. Some programs and centers already have these teams assembled.

The most important factor I used in choosing my medical team was trust. I had to trust my doctors completely, I had to believe wholeheartedly that they wanted to see me well as much as I did. Everything I told my doctors was the truth and I had to believe everything they told me was the truth.

I couldn't have trusted any doctor without being aware of his or her work. Knowing that your oncologist (cancer specialist) is board-certified (approved by the American Medical Association board in his/her subspecialty) should provide an element of comfort. Today, there are over one million new cases of cancer diagnosed yearly in the United States, but only fourteen thousand board-certified oncologists. Because of this, cancer patients are naturally being treated by doctors who specialize in other areas. To find out whether or not a physician is board-certified, you can check with the American Medical Association, any of the comprehensive cancer centers, the National Cancer Institute, or the American Society of Clinical Oncology. Or call your county's medical society for a referral. I had the opportunity to interview all my doctors prior to treatment. If you don't have that same advantage, find *one* doctor you trust completely and ask for his or her advice.

I had to like my doctors. This is not to say that I had to become close personal friends with them. If you recall, Suzy felt she had to make her doctors close personal friends and I have always thought that, that worked to her disadvantage. Having said that, it just so happened that the person I chose to be my head coach, or team leader, was George Blumenschein, my oncologist. He was and is a good friend and business associate, but that's because we have had the opportunity to develop that kind of a relationship over many years. The doctors you choose to make up your team have got to be willing to spend time with you, particularly the person you choose as your team leader.

If George Blumenschein was my head coach, I was the quarterback. I listened to him and the other members of the team and studied their advice, but I insisted on calling the shots. Of course, I was *capable* of calling the shots, because I was an educated cancer patient. You can be one too.

I also had two breast surgeons on my team, Fred Ames and George Peters. I was well aware of Fred Ames' work through the time I spent in Houston at M.D. Anderson with Suzy, although she was not his patient. I had interviewed him several times for work with the Foundation and knew his work to be first-rate. Fred Ames was the person who performed my mastectomy. George Peters, a breast surgeon in Dallas, where I live, was always willing to answer any question I might have at any time. He was very helpful to me when I labored with lymphedema, guiding me to find a way to overcome the problem rather than just accepting it. Before making these two men a part of my team, I not only interviewed them but I also spoke to some of their patients. (If you need help finding a certified breast surgeon, consult the American College of Surgeons.) Besides the two breast surgeons, I also had two plastic surgeons on the team. Being an informed cancer patient, I knew that down the line, reconstructive surgery would be in my best interest, although I wanted to allow enough time to pass to ensure that I had made a good recovery from my initial surgery. Besides the man who actually performed my surgery in Atlanta, John Bostwick, I depended on (and still depend on) a plastic surgeon in Dallas by the name of Fritz Barton for wise and sound advice. (Considerations involved in breast reconstruction and choosing a reconstructive surgeon are discussed in Chapter 7.)

Another medical member on my A Team was Dr. Marc Lippman, an oncologist and the director of the Lombardi Research Center at the Georgetown University Medical Center in Washington, D.C. I have never been a patient of his, but I greatly respect his mind and the contribution he has made to breast cancer research. Dr. Lippman has given me a thoughtful, well-thought-out answer to any question I have ever asked.

And finally, on the medical side of the team, was Dr. Stephen Jones, professor of oncology at the Charles A. Sammons Center at Baylor University Medical Center in Dallas and clinical director of the Komen Alliance. He has published extensively in the field of clinical research. He has allowed me to impose on him at any time when I've been confused or unsure. He explains things to me in clear language that I can understand—and repeat, if needed. For this reason, his influence has been immeasurable.

If you think that people of this caliber are unavailable to you, you are mistaken. Excellent help may be as close as your hospital, or at 800–I'M AWARE. (1-800-462-9273)

The Emotional Support Members

I believe that to have a winning team, a breast cancer patient needs both medical and emotional support. My requirements for the emotional support team were very much the same as for the medical support team. Each member had to have a great deal of integrity and to be honest with me at all times. I needed empathy without sympathy. I needed people who would not allow me to feel sorry for myself but rather encourage me to continue leading as normal a life as possible. My mother, Ellie Goodman, played a key role in my emotional survival. Without her nurturing every step of the way, I don't know how I would have gotten through the whole ordeal. She never left my side for a moment.

I also received a great deal of strength from talking with other breast cancer patients. There are many women out there who have given me hope and inspiration without even knowing it. *No one* can fully understand exactly what you are going through unless they have been through it themselves. It is important to seek out positive role models if you are going to get strength from other cancer patients. A positive role model is not necessarily a woman who has beaten the disease, but rather a woman who has never given up her will to live. A positive role model has learned to appreciate life *because of* having breast cancer rather than *in spite of* it. In that way, the late Jill Ireland was and will always be a role model for me, as was my dear friend the late Nina Hyde, fashion editor of *The Washington Post*. Even when their breast cancer was far advanced, both these women never gave up or gave in. Another was the late Rose Kushner, a former cancer patient and one of the guiding and leading resources in breast cancer research in this country until her death in January 1990. She not only answered my questions but always left me with a provocative thought to ponder long after our conversation ended. Rose Kushner helped me become a stronger cancer survivor.

Another member of my nonmedical support team was my good friend, Sharon McCutchin. Besides being an active member of the Komen Foundation, Sharon is the one person I can *always* count on for a good laugh. Even in my darkest, ugliest moments, she had the ability to cut through my turmoil and bring a smile to my face. I call friends who accept you without makeup and without hair *low* maintenance friends—the best kind to have!

The last two members of my emotional support A Team were my husband, Norman, and son, Eric. Norman is my best friend. He also, without ever trying and perhaps never knowing, inspired me to try to look good throughout my illness. I never wanted him to know how sick I felt, because I didn't want to scare him. Every day I made a conscious effort to fix my hair (or wig, or scarf, or turban) and put on my lipstick so that he would still find me attractive. If I wasn't up to getting dressed, I put on something colorful. Doing these little things made me feel better and if Norman wasn't around, I might not have made the effort. Eric, of course, loves me unconditionally. To this day, an evening doesn't go by without his *telling me* he loves me. I think that is a lot to get from a teen-age boy. He, above all else, provided me with the reason to get well, and get well fast.

Your A Team

That was my A Team. Once again, what worked for me may not necessarily work for you. Every one of these people was my partner. Those you choose to support you through your illness should have personalities that blend with yours. Your team should consist of the best possible medical advisors you can find, a few people who will love you no matter what you say or do, at least one person who will make you laugh, someone who pushes you to your fullest mental potential, someone who pushes you to your fullest physical potential, and someone for whom you will always want to look pretty. Once your team is set, together you can plan your winning strategy.

A Word on Doctor/Patient Relationships

Gone are the days when we, as women, must accept whatever is said to us without question or confrontation, especially where our health is concerned. As I said at the beginning of this chapter, the best thing you can do for yourself is to ask your doctor as many questions as you need to ask in order to fully understand what has happened, what is happening, and what will happen to your body. Asking questions will also aid in the evolution of good doctor/patient relationships based on understanding and open communication. As the century closes, I see a significant increase in our opportunity to make informed decisions based on our increased education and knowledge. You not only have the right to know the reason for every piece of medical advice you receive, it is now your *responsibility* to know. It is my opinion that once doctors get used to the idea of communicating openly and honestly, they will appreciate sharing the burden of the crucial decisions that must be made daily in dealing with cancer patients. Giving physicians the power to make these critical decisions without the input of their patients may have done wonders for their egos, but it has to have been murder on their stress levels.

The Questioning Process

In developing a successful relationship with your doctor, keep in mind that he or she must be treated with the same respect you insist upon for yourself. Remember that doctors are professionals. Naturally, if you are diagnosed with breast cancer you will have many urgent questions that need to be answered. The best way to handle this, I have found, is to write your questions down and try, as much as possible, to ask all your questions in one sitting. It isn't fair to call your doctor several times a day with questions or to ask for medical advice at a social get-together.

Sometimes a woman can be so preoccupied with the fact that she has cancer that it is nearly impossible for her to remember the answers to the questions she has so painstakingly prepared. This is a normal reaction and one that should not cause any undue embarrassment. What it does call for is a back-up plan. Take notes. Or bring a tape recorder into your doctor's office so you can play the tape containing both your questions and the answers later, at a time when you feel more relaxed and better able to hold onto the information. Another option might be to bring a relative or close friend into the consultation with whom you can discuss the outcome later to make sure you both received the same information.

The important thing is that you *ask* those questions no matter how frightened you are of the answers, no matter how uncomfortable it is to discuss a subject as intimate as your breasts with a virtual stranger.

What questions should you ask? I can give you a guideline, a place to begin. You can and should add to this list whatever else you want to know. No question is silly or stupid when you are fighting for your life.

1. What, specifically, did my biopsy show?
2. What surgical procedures are used to treat breast cancer?
3. What are the potential risks and benefits of these procedures?
4. Which procedure are you recommending for me, and why?
5. Where will the surgical scar or scars be located?
6. How can I expect to look and feel after surgery?
7. Why do doctors take lymph nodes from the armpit area?
8. When will you know about my lymph node involvement?
9. What role does lymph node involvement play in my overall health picture?
10. Is there any indication that my cancer has spread?
11. What were the results of my hormone receptor assays? (Your doctor may not have the results for seven to fourteen days.) What treatment is indicated by those results?
12. What about the aggressiveness of my tumor? How quickly is it growing? What factors helped you to determine this? What does this mean in terms of treatment?
13. Will I need any treatment beyond surgery? Why (or why not)? What supplemental treatments are available?

These are just a few of the first things you will probably want to know as soon as breast cancer has been diagnosed. After a specific treatment has been suggested, I'm sure you will have a lot more questions. As we discuss the different treatment options in the next chapter, I will add to that list of questions just as you will.

Speaking in Positives

The first question that comes to every woman's mind when she is told she has breast cancer is *Am I going to die?* For many years, cancer and death were two words that went hand in hand. This is not the case anymore.

More people are surviving cancer every day. Breast cancer, detected in its earliest stages, has a high percentage of successful outcomes. Asking if you are going to die, though it is an understandable question, is a difficult question for any doctor to answer. It is also very negative and immediately presents an unfavorable state of mind. To put yourself in a more positive state, try to ask questions such as: What can *I* do to beat this? or What can *we* do as a *team* to ensure my best chances of survival? You have every reason to feel hopeful about getting through this. If you want more constructive answers, ask more constructive questions.

Still, you need to know the facts. No doctor is doing you a favor if he glosses over the seriousness of your condition. But wouldn't you rather think that you have an 85 percent chance of survival than a 15 percent chance of death? Even if I was told I had a 10 percent chance of survival, *that's* what I would hold on to. When you get into the habit of speaking in positives about your condition, it will do wonders for your morale, your relationship with your doctors, and your ability to communicate openly with your family and friends. You will become a positive role model to other cancer patients without ever being conscious of it—perhaps at a time when you may have even considered giving up.

Second Opinions

Once you've prepared your questions, listened to the answers, and discussed them thoroughly, what happens if you are not satisfied with the information you've received? Are you stuck? Let me tell you about my friend Richard Bloch in Kansas City. You may have heard of him, as he is the cofounder of H & R Block, the income tax specialists. Fifteen years ago, Richard was diagnosed with what was said to be "terminal and untreatable" lung cancer, caused by many years of smoking. His surgeon told him to go home and get his will and estate together, because there was no hope. Well, that was not the answer he wanted to hear. Richard and his wife, Annette, furiously researched the disease. Because of its reputation and willingness to help him, he checked himself into M.D. Anderson Cancer Center. After undergoing radiation therapy, chemotherapy, surgery, immune-system stimulation, and psychotherapy, Richard learned that his condition was indeed treatable. "There is no type of cancer for which there is no treatment and there is no type of cancer from which some people have not been cured," he insists.

There is a lesson in Richard Bloch's story for all of us. Asking for a second opinion should never make you feel uncomfortable in any way.

Whenever cancer is involved, the situation is serious. Sometimes even a third or fourth opinion is necessary before you feel secure about both the diagnosis and the prescribed treatment. Most doctors welcome the support of their peers. If the opinions differ, the only thing that should matter to any doctor is your health. If you don't understand the diagnosis and/or treatment you've been prescribed, you will never be able to fight with the determination and gusto needed to beat this disease. Just think, after literally receiving the death sentence from one doctor, Richard Bloch has had fifteen more years of quality life and is still going strong. Doesn't that sound like a great reason to ask for a second opinion? Today, in an effort to reduce the high cost of medical treatment, many insurance companies insist on and pay for a second opinion before agreeing to underwrite any form of treatment at all.

Teamwork

The most important aspect of establishing a successful doctor/patient relationship is teamwork. I can't stress it enough. The reason cancer is such a dangerous disease is that it is difficult to control. Knowing exactly what is going on and having a say in your treatment is the only way of getting back some of the control your cancer has taken away. Regardless of how brilliant a reputation a doctor has established, if the doctor did not allow me to be a partner in my treatment, I'd find a new one. I think you should too. On the other hand, you can't be a good partner unless you make an effort to gain as much knowledge as you need from as many sources as possible. Many doctors have gotten into the habit of making all the decisions because *we have allowed them to make all of our decisions.* If you feel your doctor is worth keeping, but he doesn't know how to make you a partner, *teach him.*

Dr. Marc Lippman describes doctor/patient relationships this way: "Imagine you are in a department store and the clerk seems anxious to help you, knowing and expecting you to be a motivated buyer. He or she seems willing to walk the aisles with you, explore the drawers and bins for obscure merchandise, or call the warehouse to see if there is anything new on order which may suit you better. This is the spirit you should expect from your doctor." Genuine concern for your recovery, genuine desire to find the most appropriate form of treatment for your particular case, and genuine likability—it's not too much to ask.

CHAPTER SIX

Knowing Your Treatment Options

I very sincerely wish you would exert yourself so as to keep all your matters in order yourself without depending on others as that is the only way to be happy and to have all your business in your own hands.

—MARTHA WASHINGTON

Once you have been diagnosed with breast cancer, you must find out what all your options are so you can discuss them intelligently with your doctor, your family, and your friends. But before you and your doctor can discuss the options, you must both be aware of the specifics of your particular cancer, what stage it is in and how far, if at all, it has metastasized (spread). Your doctor will recommend other tests such as X rays and blood tests, and surgical removal of some or all of the underarm lymph nodes to determine just how far your breast cancer has progressed.

A chest X ray will check to see if the cancer has spread to the lungs and bone X rays will look at the ribs, back, and hips and other parts of the skeleton. The blood tests will determine the status of the liver, kidneys, and other organs. You should ask your doctor what X rays and blood tests he or she is recommending, what information he or she hopes to obtain, and, after completion, what the results of these tests have shown.

One of the most important factors in determining the stage of the cancer is whether or not the underarm, or axillary, lymph nodes have been invaded by the cancer. This information is obtained by surgically removing some of the lymph nodes. If your breast is removed (a mastectomy), the lymph nodes are routinely removed along with the breast. If you are a candidate for breast preservation and only a portion of your breast is removed in a lumpectomy, the lymph nodes under the arm are usually removed through a separate incision. In either case, the doctors will know if the lymph nodes are involved, and if so, how many.

The following staging system is used to describe the progress of breast cancer.

- *CARCINOMA IN SITU OR LOCALIZED CANCER:* very early breast cancer which is present only in the immediate area in which it began, with no evidence of tissue invasion.

- *STAGE I:* means the tumor is no longer than 2 centimeters (about 1 inch) in diameter and has not spread (metastasized) outside the breast or to the lymph nodes.

- *STAGE II:* means the tumor is from 2 to 5 centimeters (approximately 1 to 2 inches) and/or has spread (metastasized) to the lymph nodes under the arm.

- *STAGE III:* means the cancer is larger than 5 centimeters (more than 2 inches) and involves the underarm lymph nodes to a greater extent and/or has spread to other lymph nodes or other tissues near the breast.

- *STAGE IV:* means the cancer has metastasized to other organs of the body, most often the lungs, bones, liver, or brain.

Standard Treatments

There are four standard forms of treatment for breast cancer: surgery, radiation therapy, chemotherapy, and hormone therapy. Beyond that, there is exciting new hope for breast cancer patients being researched as I write. Surgery and radiation are local forms of treatment, affecting only the cells in the treated area. Chemotherapy and hormone therapy are systemic forms of treatment, affecting cancer cells and noncancerous cells throughout the body by circulating through the bloodstream and the lymphatic system. In order to treat all aspects of the disease, doctors often prescribe a combination of treatments. Usually surgery is the primary treatment, or first option, and the other three are used as follow-up, or adjuvant, therapy. The course of treatment your doctor suggests will depend on several different factors such as tumor type, stage, and location, your age, and your medical history.

It is standard today to be treated by a team of medical experts including an oncologist, a surgeon (or a surgical oncologist), a radiation therapist, and a pathologist. (A pathologist studies tissue removed from your body to determine if cancer cells are present, and if they are, what kind of cancer

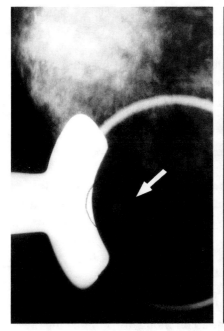
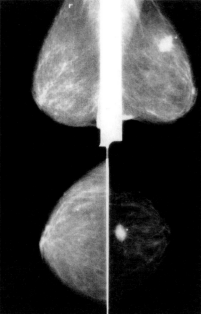

(18)

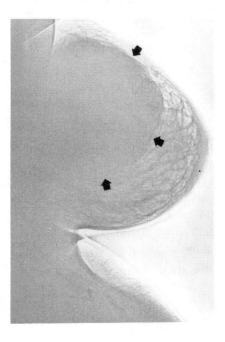

A mammogram is crucial in detecting and defining cancers of various sizes. (17) Carcinoma in situ, a very early breast cancer, side view. The arrow points out the barely discernible growth, approximately ⅕ inch.
(18) Stage 1 breast cancer, approximately 1 inch, side view.
(19) Large breast cancer, side view. The arrows define the cancerous mass. (PHOTOS COURTESY OF DR. GEORGE PETERS)

cells.) You may not actually see all these people, but they will be working together to determine your treatment.

Your personal feelings about each treatment option, and how it fits in with your lifestyle and your self-image, are immensely important. Be honest with your doctor and tell him or her exactly how you feel as you discuss each possibility.

Surgery

Surgery is most often the primary treatment for breast cancer. Its purpose is to remove the cancer and ultimately stop the growth of the disease before it has the chance to spread. If you are a Stage IV cancer patient, surgery may not be recommended, depending on the extent to which the cancer has spread. This does not mean that there isn't a treatment for you; it only means that surgery would not be in your best interest as, once again, the purpose of surgery is ultimately to prevent the disease from spreading beyond the breast to other parts of the body through the lymphatic system and the bloodstream. If your breast cancer has significantly metastasized, there is no point in putting your body through the trauma of surgery.

There are several types of surgery now commonly used in treating breast cancer. You should discuss all of them thoroughly with your A Team and decide together which procedure best fulfills your medical and psychological needs. Naturally, the first question most women have is, Can my breast be saved? This is a normal question, an understandable question, but should be second to the question, *Can my life be saved?*

TYPES OF SURGICAL PROCEDURES

- RADICAL MASTECTOMY: removal of the entire breast, the underarm lymph nodes, and the major and minor pectoral muscles and the lining over them. My Aunt Rose had a radical mastectomy, also known as the Halsted radical mastectomy (named after the doctor, William Halsted, who developed it in 1882), and if you recall, she was terribly disfigured. Although this operation was standard procedure for about seventy years, it is rarely performed in this country anymore unless the breast cancer has spread to the major pectoral muscles.

- MODIFIED RADICAL MASTECTOMY: the most common form of breast cancer surgery done at this time, though the lumpectomy is quickly gaining ground as a favored surgical treatment. It is also referred to as a total mastectomy with axillary dissection, meaning that the entire breast is removed along with the underarm lymph nodes, the lining over the chest muscles, and sometimes the minor pectoral muscles. The major pectoral muscle is left intact, making it easier to flex and rotate the arm during and after recovery. The modified radical mastectomy is a vast improvement over the radical mastectomy also because when the major chest muscle is left in place, a woman has much more freedom of movement, her surgery is not as obvious while wearing a prosthesis, and reconstruction is more cosmetically effective.

- *MODIFIED RADICAL MASTECTOMY FOLLOWED BY IMMEDIATE RECONSTRUCTION:* a subject of some controversy. In very small cancers (carcinoma in situ), having reconstructive surgery at the time of the mastectomy is thought to be quite safe. In larger cancers, many doctors feel it is in the patient's best interest to wait and observe the results of the mastectomy before beginning reconstruction because if the cancer is not thoroughly removed or if it recurs, the reconstruction will make it difficult to detect.

- *LUMPECTOMY FOLLOWED BY RADIATION:* also known as tylectomy. This procedure removes the cancerous tumor plus a rim of surrounding normal tissue. Surgery is followed by radiation therapy. Usually, during surgery some of the underarm lymph nodes are removed and tested as well. If there is lymph node involvement, additional therapy will probably be required such as chemotherapy and/or hormone therapy. The advantage of the lumpectomy is that the breast is saved, often making the disease easier to handle psychologically. The disadvantages of the lumpectomy known at this time are that on small-breasted women the procedure can cause noticeable disfigurement and the scar tissue surrounding the treated area can make both physical exams and future mammograms more difficult to interpret. Even so, at this time in this country, lumpectomy and removal of lymph nodes under the arm followed by radiation is the most common and preferred form of breast preservation. At a Consensus Conference of the National Cancer Institute in June 1990, the expert panel concluded that lumpectomy, removal of the axillary lymph nodes, and X-ray therapy is the *preferred* procedure over modified radical mastectomy. The important thing to remember is that current data suggests that the survival rates with lumpectomy versus mastectomy are virtually the same.

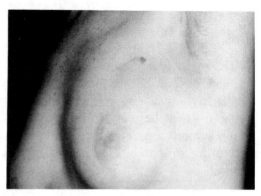

(20) Lumpectomy and underarm lymph node removal, the most common form of breast preservation. (PHOTO COURTESY OF DR. GEORGE PETERS)

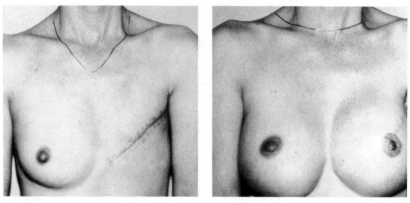

(21) Modified radical mastectomy, currently the most common form of breast cancer surgery, followed by breast reconstruction with tissue expansion. (PHOTO COURTESY OF DR. JOHN BOSTWICK)

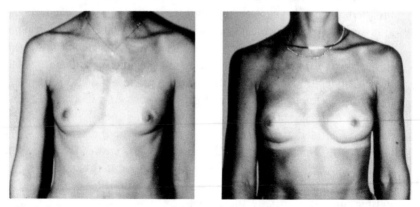

(22) Subcutaneous mastectomy and immediate reconstruction with implants. (PHOTO COURTESY OF DR. JOHN BOSTWICK)

- *SEGMENTAL MASTECTOMY FOLLOWED BY RADIATION:* also known as a partial mastectomy. This procedure removes the tumor plus a wedge of the unaffected surrounding tissue and a small portion of the overlying skin and lining of the chest muscle around the tumor. Most often this surgery also includes removal of several of the underarm lymph nodes to check for the possible spread of the cancer. Surgery is followed by radiation therapy. As in the case of the lumpectomy, if the disease has metastasized to the nodes, other forms of treatment will most likely be discussed. For large-breasted women, this may prove to have good cosmetic results, but it is not preferred treatment in breast preservation. This procedure is a minor variation of the lumpectomy procedure.

- *QUADRANTECTOMY FOLLOWED BY RADIATION:* removal of the quarter of the breast containing the tumor plus the skin covering the major pectoral muscle, the entire minor pectoral muscle, and the underarm lymph nodes. This surgery is usually accompanied by radiation therapy. Like the segmental mastectomy, the quadrantectomy may be beneficial to large-breasted women in saving their breast, but for smaller-breasted women, this procedure will not have a pretty cosmetic result. It is not preferred treatment.

CONSIDERATIONS

When determining your surgical, or primary, treatment, two factors are taken into consideration above all others: first, which form of surgery will most likely ensure your best chance of recovery, and second, which form of surgery will most likely give the best possible cosmetic results (appearance). Modified radical mastectomy is the most commonly prescribed primary treatment. However, recent studies are showing that the survival rate of women with Stage I or Stage II breast cancer treated with a lumpectomy followed by radiation therapy is equal that of those with a mastectomy. For some, the fear of losing a breast can be more traumatic than the fear of cancer itself. This fear is what keeps many women from mammography screening and from practicing breast self-exam. For that reason alone, the advancement of the lumpectomy has been invaluable. Knowing that the discovery of breast cancer does not have to mean the automatic loss of the breast may bring more women to a psychological place where they can be aggressive about their breast health.

However, two women with the exact same size cancerous lesion will not necessarily benefit from the exact same surgery. Remember, I had a very small malignancy in my left breast, but because of its location, a lumpectomy was not my best option. The cosmetic results of a lumpectomy would have been more disfiguring than those of a modified radical mastectomy followed by breast reconstruction. A woman with very small breasts or a tumor located close to the nipple has to think carefully about what procedure will be better for her in the long run. Sometimes even if a lumpectomy is a clinical option, it is not the best cosmetic option.

As you can see, the surgical options you have are quite varied. Which surgery is right for you will become obvious after discussing your test results with your team of doctors. Because of the recent NCI Consensus Conference, lumpectomy and radiation will be more often recommended in the years to come.

Radiation

The purpose of radiation therapy is to destroy by the use of high-energy X rays directed to a particular location any remaining cancer cells in the breast or lymph nodes that were not removed during surgery. Whereas at one time, radiation therapy was used mainly to treat patients with advanced cancer, now, with the development of the lumpectomy and other breast-conservation operations, radiation has proved quite successful as adjuvant therapy in the early stages of breast cancer. *Lumpectomy without radiation therapy is a poor choice of treatment.* There is as much as a 30 percent chance of cancer recurrence if the lumpectomy is performed without the radiation follow-up. Today, chemotherapy and hormone therapy are also considered to be adjuvant therapies after a mastectomy, and some doctors will prescribe a combination of several different treatments when the size, location, and aggressiveness of the cancer warrant it.

If you and your surgeon have opted for lumpectomy and radiation therapy, it is very important to see the radiation oncologist (a physician who specializes in the use of high-energy X rays to treat cancer) in consultation before your surgery. Because the radiation oncologist will be providing X ray treatment after the surgery, it is necessary for him or her to be in complete agreement that you are a good candidate for this form of therapy.

After your surgery and lymph node removal are completed, you will need a week or two to heal and prepare emotionally for the next round of treatment. Your first visit to the radiation oncologist will not entail any treatment at all, but rather give you an opportunity to discuss your treatment plan openly and ask any questions you might have regarding the procedure. Together you and the doctor will discuss how the radiation will be given, where exactly the radiation will be given, and how many treatments will be required. Usually, radiation treatments are given five days a week, for five weeks straight.

Also during that first visit, ink lines are drawn on the body to mark the exact area that the radiation will be aimed. The ink is permanent and will not wash off in the bath or shower, but will naturally fade away in time. Do not attempt to scrub it off because following the ink lines is the only way to be sure that the treatment is delivered in the exact same area every day.

The room in which the radiation will actually be administered can be a bit intimidating at first. You will lie on a metal table under a large machine—perhaps a linear accelerator or a cobalt machine (more on this later)—from which the radiation is dispersed. The technician will spend as much time as it takes to ensure that you are in just the right position. It is of the utmost importance that you do not move after you have been correctly positioned because the entire procedure would be useless if the radiation misses the intended tissue. The technician will then leave the room to avoid exposure to the radiation and you will be observed through a closed-circuit television. The radiation therapist will consult with the dosimetrist, the person who computes and regulates the radiation dosage. The standard dosage given for early stage breast cancer is somewhere between 4400 and 5000 rads.

Radiation therapy does not hurt, but there are a few common side effects you may or may not experience in the treated area such as itching, redness, tanning, or sunburn. The treated area may also become firm and/or rough to the feel. Many women are fatigued during radiation therapy, so it is important to get enough rest and to eat nutritiously in order to keep up your strength. Each of these side effects can be annoying, but they will pass when your treatment is completed. There are a few more serious side effects which are far less common. Because the lungs, heart, and ribs are located in such close proximity to the breasts, they unavoidably receive minimal amounts of radiation. Although it happens rarely, this exposure can cause radiation-induced pneumonia, pericardial effusion, which is fluid around the heart, or rib fractures.

As is the case with any breast cancer treatment, radiation can fail to stop the recurrence of the cancer, requiring a mastectomy at a later date. However, studies show that most women treated for breast cancer by primary radiation therapy after lumpectomy are as pleased with the outcome cosmetically as they are with the improved survival rate and prognosis.

RADIATION BOOST

Approximately two weeks after the external radiation therapy has been completed, almost all women will receive what is called a booster dose of radiation, either externally using an electron beam or internally using an iridium implant. The external booster is being used more often these days, but the implant is still used occasionally. The purpose of the booster is to give the treated area one last shot of radiation before ending the treatment. It is, in fact, a precautionary procedure which attempts to ensure that all the cancer cells have been destroyed.

The beam boost is produced through a type of linear accelerator machine, very similar to the one used in the original treatment, aimed directly at the site of the original tumor. It will require five consecutive days of treatment. If you have your boost by beam, do not be concerned if you see additional redness or irritation; this is quite normal.

The implant procedure will require a short hospital stay, probably no more than two or three days, and be done usually under general anesthesia. Thin plastic tubes are threaded through the tissue where the original tumor was taken out. How many tubes are used depends on the size and location of the tumor that was removed. To make sure that the tubes are correctly in place, a chest X ray will be taken. Then you will be taken back to your room, where the radioactive material (iridium) is inserted into the plastic tubes.

During these two or three days, you will receive approximately 2000 rads to the site of the original tumor and surrounding tissue. The procedure is not painful, although you may experience slight discomfort at the time the tubes are being put in place and removed, much like the feeling of stitches being put in and taken out. This discomfort can be minimized with medication.

You will not be confined to your bed but will be able to move around the room freely. It is necessary to stay in a private room because the implant emits small amounts of radiation which may possibly put other people in the room at risk. Visitors must stay at least six feet away and it is not recommended that children or pregnant women enter the room at all.

This is just a precaution, as the amount of radiation received by visitors is not thought to be large enough to be a health risk. After the two or three days, the plastic tubes will be removed and you will be discharged from the hospital.

CONSIDERATIONS
You will probably have a lot of questions about radiation before you can commit to this form of treatment. Just the name alone can be frightening. Here is a list of possible questions you may want to ask during your initial consultation. There are probably other questions you will want to add to the list. Ask as many questions as you need, and keep asking until you have enough information to make an informed decision.

1. What is radiation therapy?
2. After reading my pathology report, viewing the slides, and examining me, do you feel the size, location, and type of tumor I have will be responsive to radiation therapy? Will you explain why (or why not)?
3. How does the radiation work?
4. Are normal tissues damaged in the process?
5. What is the course time and dosage of radiation therapy?
6. How often will I be seen by a physician during the course of treatment?
7. What kind of machine will be used, linear accelerator or cobalt? What are the advantages and disadvantages of each?
8. How reliable is the machine? How often is it unable to function? How old is the machine?
9. Who administers the treatment? If it is a technician, how experienced is he or she? How closely is he or she supervised?
10. How long does each treatment take?
11. Should I come alone, or should a friend or relative accompany me?
12. What side effects might occur, and how long do they last? Which side effects should be reported to the doctor or nurse?
13. Would any special diet or dietary supplement eliminate or lessen the side effects?

14. Are follow-up visits with a physician necessary upon completion of therapy? How often are check-ups and tests required after completion?

15. I understand that ink markings last for months, leaving residue on clothing. Can you use tattoos if I prefer? What does tattooing involve?

16. What are the precautions or prohibitions during and after treatment (e.g., use of skin creams and lotion, underam shaving, etc.)?

17. Is it all right to continue normal activities such as work, sex, and sports during and after treatment?

18. How soon should treatment begin? What are the risks if I delay or miss a treatment?

19. Do you recommend other forms of treatment in conjunction with radiation therapy? Why (or why not)?

20. What is the cost of radiation therapy? Is it usually covered by medical insurance? (Check your own policy's terms.)

Chemotherapy

Chemotherapy is the treatment of cancer with cytotoxic drugs—that is, drugs that literally kill fast-growing cells, which is what cancer is all about (a short, uncomplicated definition of cancer being the rapid, uncontrolled, abnormal growth of cells). Since chemotherapy is a systemic treatment— the drugs circulate in the body through the lymphatic system and the bloodstream—unlike surgery and radiation, it can reach tiny cancer cells that have broken away from solid tumors and spread to distant sites which may be undetectable by currently available tests. For this reason, chemotherapy is invaluable as a weapon against cancer. Today, it is being used earlier and earlier in cancer treatment in addition to surgery and radiation in the attempt to prevent or postpone a cancer recurrence.

Chemotherapy can be administered into a vein (IV) (either one in the arm or through a specialized type of venous access catheter—there are several types of these and you should ask your doctor), or orally through pills.

Like every other form of cancer treatment, however, chemotherapy has its own set of disadvantages. Because it cannot, as of yet, distinguish between fast-growing cancer cells and fast-growing "normal" cells in the body, there are many potential side effects associated with chemotherapy. The most obvious are loss of hair, loss of energy, nausea, vomiting, and susceptibility to infection. There are others, as well, which may or may not occur depending on your particular prescription and dosage, such as deterioration of bone marrow, mouth ulcers, rashes, changes in skin pigment, blood in the urine caused by bladder inflammation, lung damage, and weakness of the heart. And like any other form of cancer treatment, there is always the possibility that chemotherapy will not work—in this case because the body builds up a tolerance for or immunity to the drugs.

Experiments and studies are being done every day to improve the effectiveness of chemotherapy while diminishing its side effects. There is also a great effort being made to simplify the form of treatment so that women on chemotherapy can continue with their regular lifestyles as much as possible.

TYPES OF CHEMOTHERAPEUTIC DRUGS

There are many different drugs used in a variety of combinations being employed to treat all kinds of cancer. The good news is that many of these drugs are effective in treating breast cancer. Let's go over each of them so that when you and your oncologist discuss them, they won't seem completely foreign.

- *ALKYLATING AGENTS:* kill tumor cells by interfering with the cell's building blocks, called DNA. Examples of alkylating agents are melphalan (Alkeran), cyclophosphamide (Cytoxan), chlorambucil (Leukeran), nitrogen mustard (Mustargen), and Thiotepa.

- *PLANT ALKALOIDS:* also work on keeping the cells from dividing. These chemotherapeutic agents, which come from the periwinkle plant, have proven effective in treating breast cancer. Some examples of plant alkaloids are vincristine sulfate (Oncovin) and vinblastine (Velban).

- *ANTIMETABOLITES:* work by interfering with the cancer cell's ability to produce RNA and DNA and are especially effective in killing dividing cells. Examples of antimetabolites effective in treating breast cancer are 5-Fluorouracil (5-FU) and methotrexate.

- *ANTIBIOTICS:* have a completely different meaning when being used in the treatment of cancer than when used in the treatment of infections, because in this case the antibiotics destroy tumor cells, not bacteria. Doxorubicin (Adriamycin) and mutamycin (Mitomycin C) have proven particularly effective in treating breast cancer.

These are just a few of the most common drugs you are likely to hear about when discussing chemotherapy; you may hear of others. Try not to be alarmed by the sound of their names. Remember, scientists and doctors have a language of their own. Each drug has its specific purpose and you have a right to know exactly what is going into your body and why. If you don't understand what a term means, don't be embarrassed to ask. Without having made a scientific study of the names of drugs, how are you to know what they mean?

CONSIDERATIONS

We are currently in the middle of what has been dubbed "the chemo controversy." It is in your best interest to understand it and make up your own mind as to which side of the fence you stand on. There are those who believe the unpleasant side effects of chemotherapy are not worth its potential value, at least in some cases. Just as the Halsted radical mastectomy has been all but eliminated as a standard surgical option for breast cancer patients today, some say aggressive (high-dosage) chemotherapy is just as outdated and should ultimately be eliminated as well.

My friend the late Rose Kushner, former head of the Breast Cancer Advisory Center, author of two in-depth books on the disease, co-founder of NABCO (National Alliance of Breast Cancer Organizations), and a breast cancer patient herself, felt strongly that aggressive chemotherapy is a barbaric method of treating women and causes as much physical and emotional suffering as does the disease itself.

Rose and I differed somewhat on the subject. Although neither one of us is or was a doctor, we were both cancer patients who made careers out of the disease. I believe to get the best results from chemotherapy, a woman must be given it early in the treatment course and to maximum dosage. Unfortunately for the patient in our country, each onocologist develops a preferred drug regimen. But dosage tinkering is not in the patient's best interest. There is good data today on the amounts of drugs that are effective. There are also new drugs and combinations of drugs being used at this time that will not cause the hair to fall out or upset the stomach. So far, these drugs have not been proven as successful in treating the cancer. I wish there were a way to eliminate it, but right now losing your hair is a frequent side effect to chemotherapy. All forms of chemotherapy are cytotoxic. If you have made the commitment to go through the treatment, why not fight the disease with the most powerful weapons available in full dosage?

The side effects of chemotherapy are almost always temporary, but occasionally they aren't. It is a risk every cancer patient must face. I personally think the risk is worth taking. Only when we see confirmed proof that milder dosages of chemotherapy are as effective as the strongest dosages in preventing a breast cancer recurrence, will I support them.

However, you have to make your own choices. Sometimes the quality of life, even in shorter time increments, is more important than the quantity of life. This largely depends on the stage of a particular cancer, the age of the patient, and the patient's lifestyle. What was right for me may not be right for you. We all have to respect the individual choices made by each cancer patient. I just want to make sure that every woman with breast cancer understands the seriousness of the disease and is aware of all the options she has available to choose from. Breast cancer is a formidable opponent. To win the war, you have got to fight.

Here is a list of common questions most often asked when chemotherapy is prescribed. Use it as a guideline and add to it whatever you need in order to have a better understanding of your treatment.

1. What, specifically, is chemotherapy, and why is it indicated in my case?
2. What is the significance of lymph node involvement in relation to chemotherapy?
3. How many of my nodes were involved?
4. What were the results of my hormone receptor assays and my flow cytometry test? What other tests did you run? How did the results of these tests influence your treatment suggestions?
5. Which chemotherapy drugs are you recommending for me? Why have you chosen those particular drugs rather than another combination?
6. How many months will I need this treatment?
7. How frequent are the treatments?
8. How are the drugs administered?
9. Will I have to go to the hospital for treatment?
10. How long does each treatment take?
11. Should I come alone for the treatments, or should a friend or relative accompany me?

12. Tell me all of the possible side effects I might experience. Are they permanent? Does everyone get them?
13. Is there anything I can do to lessen or relieve the side effects?
14. How much do these treatments cost? Will they be covered by my health insurance?

Chemotherapy has proven its effectiveness in putting some cancer patients in complete remission. Other times it doesn't work at all; still other times it can add a few good years to a woman's life. To me, knowing all the risks, enduring this often unpleasant form of treatment was worth every minute of suffering I experienced, though at times during the treatment I might not have admitted it. You must think about all the benefits, weigh them against the negatives, and decide for yourself what is best for you.

Hormone Therapy

Like chemotherapy, hormone therapy is a systemic treatment. Unlike chemotherapy, it is not cytotoxic—it does not kill cancer cells directly. Hormones are substances naturally produced by the endocrine glands. Their purpose is to stimulate other organs. Hormones are largely responsible for reproductive functions (such as ovulation and milk production) and for aspects of appearance that distinguish the sexes. When cancer begins in tissues that are affected by hormones, such as the breasts, it is possible the tumor will be affected by hormones as well. In premenopausal women, drugs that suppress female hormones (estrogen and progesterone) may also suppress the growth of cancer. In postmenopausal women, other types of hormones may have the same effect.

Originally, hormone therapy as a treatment for breast cancer was limited to the surgical removal of hormone-producing glands, as in an oophorectomy (the removal of the ovaries). Today, however, while surgery to remove the ovaries may be desirable in treating cases where the production of hormones by the body is believed to be speeding up tumor growth, synthetic drugs such as tamoxifen, megestrol acetate, or aminoglutethamide plus hydrocortisone have been proven to control recurrent breast cancer and produce long remissions from the disease as well. Once again, the names of the drugs are more intimidating than the drugs themselves. The truth is that in many cases where hormone therapy is an option, the side effects are much less troublesome than with chemotherapy. In rare cases, however, hormone therapy may cause serious side effects such as depression, blood clots, or rarely, elevated levels of calcium in the blood. Very rarely, hormone therapy produces the opposite effect from that intended and the tumor growth is speeded up.

One problem with hormone therapy is that it can take up to several months to determine whether or not it is having a significant effect on the tumor. Therefore, if your cancer is posing a threat to a vital organ, chemotherapy would have to be used instead, since it works much faster.

It is crucial that a hormone receptor assay be done at the time of biopsy to determine whether or not hormone therapy is an option for you, and that you be made aware of the results. The presence of estrogen and progesterone receptors in breast cancer is thought to be associated with high survival rates and long-term remissions. However, if your hormone receptor assay proves to be negative, as was mine, you can still achieve optimal results through chemotherapy and/or radiation in conjunction with your initial breast surgery. Clearly, the best advantage of having a positive hormone receptor assay is that it gives you another option in treatment.

CONSIDERATIONS

Here are some questions you may want to know the answers to before considering hormone therapy. As always, use them along with your own questions.

1. What is hormone therapy?
2. What were the results of my hormone receptor assays?
3. How and why do they warrant this treatment?
4. Which hormone drugs are you recommending for me, and why?
5. In what form will the treatment be given, and how often will treatment be given?
6. Should I have hormone therapy in conjunction with any other forms of treatment?
7. What if hormone therapy does not work for me? What other choices do I have?
8. What are the side effects I might encounter and what, if anything, can I do to prevent them from occurring?
9. What is the cost of hormone therapy, and will it be covered by my insurance?

New Approaches to Treatment

Now that we have discussed the four standard cancer treatments, let's talk a little bit about treatments we are *not* sure of at this time: biological therapies, clinical trials, bone marrow transplant, and the so-called

Biological Therapy: The New Frontier

I refer to biological therapy as the new frontier in breast cancer research because it is exciting and offers hope for the future. Through the study of what they call biological response modifiers, scientists are now beginning to understand cancer at its most basic cellular level. This means they are getting closer to discovering what causes a normal cell to change into a cancer cell. To me this sounds like a great breakthrough. I can't help but wonder, however, what will happen thirty years from now if, in a moment of rare nostalgia, my son Eric should pick up this book with his own son or daughter and glance through the pages. Do you suppose they'll laugh at what I once thought was a great breakthrough? Probably.

Immunotherapy means just what the name indicates—an effort to stimulate the body's immune system in order to recognize and attack cancer cells. Today it is still highly experimental, though progress is being made in all forms of systemic adjuvant therapy. New substances are being tested every day. The important and positive aspect of immunotherapy is that it has been sometimes noted to benefit the advanced cancer patient as well as patients who have detected their cancers early.

Perhaps the greatest hope for the treatment of breast cancer in the future will come from therapies that are based on an improved understanding of the way in which breast cancer begins and progresses. Dr. Marc Lippman offers us the simple yet useful analogy of asking a cave man to try to stop a car's engine. If he takes out a club, there is no question that sooner or later he could get the car to stop, but by then the car would be reduced to a complete wreck. While this may be an overstated analogy for chemotherapy and radiation treatment, it is also clear that these therapies can damage normal as well as abnormal parts of the body. A more rational understanding of how a car works leads to half a dozen strategies which could conceivably stop the car without damaging it, such as turning off the ignition, siphoning out the gas, pulling off the distributor cap, etc. In the same sense, as we start to understand the specific components that set a cancer cell apart from normal cells (its ability to grow continuously in an unregulated fashion, its ability to invade normal structures and tissues, and finally, its ability to break away from the parent tumor mass and spread throughout the body), we will be able to design therapies that are directed against these factors.

Great progress has been made in the last few years in understanding the specific genes, termed oncogenes, involved in changing normal cells into cancer cells. A variety of treatments designed to work against these oncogenes has already been developed, and has been successful in the test tube. Over the next five years we will witness the first clinical trials in which the behavior of these cancer-causing genes can be observed and, ultimately, defeated. It has never been more important to pay as much attention as possible to improved screening, early detection, and the rehabilitation of breast cancer patients.

Clinical Trials and Research Studies

Clinical trials and research studies involving patients with breast cancer are important sources of information on new treatments. Much of what is used successfully in the treatment of breast cancer today comes from the clinical trials conducted in years past. These successes are in large part due to the courageous women who participated in past clinical trials. It is essential that these valuable clinical trials continue to be supported so that medical science can move closer to finding a cure. Clinical trials are important and should continue to be supported.

I was lucky. I was placed in a clinical trial that has proven to be very successful. If I had to make a choice about whether or not to participate in a clinical trial again, I would do it in a heartbeat. Some women feel that being a part of a study group makes them a "guinea pig" for scientists; I disagree. Today, medical science has become so advanced that you will always be given some form of studied treatment which will be matched against another form of proven treatment to see if there is a slight or marked edge for one over the other.

You can find out what clinical trials are being done, and where, by contacting PDQ (Physicians Data Query), a computerized information service that provides doctors and patients with the most up-to-date cancer information possible. PDQ can tell you who has the state-of-the-art facilities and where the newest tests are being conducted (see Resource section for addresses and telephone numbers). When you call, you will need to know your diagnosis, including type and stage of cancer, where the primary cancer is located, cell type, and address and phone number of the physician who is providing your treatment. The information PDQ gives you, however, is written in medical terminology that most of us will not be able to understand. It is better to tell your doctor that you have accessed PDQ and have the report sent directly to him or her. You can then go over the information together. See Resources, pages 191 and 200.

Bone Marrow Transplantation
Another promising approach in breast cancer treatment is bone marrow transplantation. In this procedure, your bone marrow cells are collected from your hips, or, with the newest techniques, in some cases taken from your bloodstream, and stored away. During bone marrow transplantation, you are given massive doses of chemotherapy to kill the cancer; then your prestored bone marrow cells are "sent in" through your blood vessels to restore the bone marrow that has been damaged by the chemotherapy.

Alternative Therapies
Rose Kushner once said, "Remember, today's quackery may be tomorrow's breakthrough!" Of course she was referring to the fact that scientists may be open-minded but need to prove theories with hard research and testing. As an active member of the National Cancer Advisory Board, I have had the distinct privilege of meeting some of the most respected scientists in the country. I have sat in on numerous panel discussions and have witnessed first-hand the genuine thrill that is felt when a breakthrough is made. I have also been around when what was thought to be a promising discovery fails in some way—everyone mourns. There is no hidden cure for cancer. When the cure *is* found, the whole world will know about it. The National Cancer Institute is always willing to listen to new ideas about breakthrough possibilities. However, all hypotheses must be tested and proved in the same strict format as is used in any other practical study. The health and safety of all people depend on it.

Alternative therapies are treatments for cancer that have not been sanctioned by the medical community's clinical trials—for example, vitamin therapy, coffee enemas, a macrobiotic diet, an all-fruit diet, homeopathic medicine, and laughter therapy. I investigated the subject with a number of doctors and some of my associates on the National Cancer Advisory Board. Just about every physician I spoke to admitted that most of their patients "do something" in addition to conventional medicine. And why not? Why shouldn't you do anything and everything you can to make yourself feel better? The problem begins when people attempt to *replace* conventional treatment with these alternative therapies.

However, although proper diet, the right vitamins, some natural herbs, and exercise are certainly helpful in keeping the body clean, fit, and healthy, so far, none of them has been proven to successfully stop or even slow down cancer. The isolated cases you may hear or read about are not, I believe, something to pin your hopes on. One to two percent of all cancer patients go into what is called spontaneous remission, cancer remission without the aid of medicine. When this happens—and it is rare—the situation is the exception, not the rule. Please don't be fooled into thinking a crazy diet or a mysterious herb is going to cure your cancer.

A woman I know who has been a good friend for a long time developed a small breast cancer two years ago and was successfully treated and reconstructed. A beautiful, energetic woman, she seemed to handle her illness with a great attitude and recovered quite quickly. She was a role model to other cancer patients. Speaking to women's groups about her experience, she helped many women. Approximately six months ago, my friend was diagnosed with a kind of lymph node cancer called lymphoma. Her doctor advised her to undergo chemotherapy, feeling her chances for a possible long-term remission were excellent. What happened between her recovery from breast cancer and her development of lymphoma, I'm not sure, but now she wanted no part of chemotherapy or any conventional medicine. She opted for a strict macrobiotic diet as her sole treatment. Afraid that she would be criticized by her friends and doctors, this woman checked into a rather well-known "cancer clinic" over the border. Well, her disease did not regress; instead it had spread throughout her body. My friend died just as this book went to press.

Perhaps none of us really knew how the treatment for breast cancer affected her. Maybe her side effects were worse than she ever let on. My friend had no children and had been through a painful divorce. She had no one for whom to fight. I feel that because she was an educated cancer patient, she simply opted for the quality of life rather than the quantity and knew in her heart what the outcome would be. I really don't believe she actually thought this diet would take the place of medical science. Still, it was her choice to make and we all must respect that whether we agree with it or not. I'm just sad because I loved this friend.

On the other hand, I am in full agreement with trying anything and everything to make the unpleasant experience more tolerable as long as your doctors are aware of what you are doing and it does not interfere with the primary and adjuvant cancer treatments. During my courses of chemotherapy, I found imaging particularly helpful. I tried to look at "the big picture" first, thinking that these few months of sickness would be minuscule compared to the rest of the healthy life I intended to live. At the times when it got really bad and I felt so sick, I thought back to childbirth. *That* was much worse. Before each treatment session I would plan a fun outing for a few days afterward. It didn't have to be anything fancy—a movie with Eric or a quiet dinner out with Norman would do just fine. When I started to feel bad, I would visualize myself already there, and I would feel better right away.

I also surrounded myself with a lot of "white light," meaning a lot of positive energy. I tried to be with only those people I knew cared deeply for me and for whom I cared deeply. I read poetry and listened to soft music. When I felt up to it, I took long walks in the sunshine and rode horses. I tried to meditate and made it a point to be thankful for my blessings. Above all, I never discounted the power of laughter or the power of prayer.

In Summary

The important thing to know about any and all forms of cancer treatment is that *you have choices*—no matter how far your cancer has progressed.

Surgery, radiation therapy, chemotherapy, and hormone therapy are constantly being tested and retested for ways of improving the process, and promising and exciting new ways of treating breast cancer are continually being studied. Research your disease. Talk to your A team. Talk to patients. Call the Susan G. Komen Breast Cancer Foundation.

CHAPTER SEVEN

Breast Reconstruction

It's always
something.

—GILDA RADNER

There are some women who choose never to have reconstruction following mastectomy. Going through surgery and/or radiation and chemotherapy may be all the trauma they would like their body to endure. Other women feel that they cannot get along without it. Knowing that reconstruction will bring back her feminine silhouette may be the determining factor in a woman's decision to go through with the mastectomy.

Clearly, the decision to have reconstructive breast surgery is very personal and depends on several important factors including age, general physical health, and self-image. Having had breast reconstruction two years after my mastectomy, I feel the best thing about reconstruction is its ability to promote a sense of wellness. Although I adjusted well psychologically to losing a breast, got used to wearing a prosthesis, and was successful in getting back to a normal life, my missing breast was a constant conscious and subconscious reminder that I had had cancer. It wasn't until after my reconstruction that I could truly begin to put the disease behind me. On one level the fact that I have had breast cancer will never be completely forgotten. In the back of my mind there is always a thought of recurrence—that's the negative. However, because my own life was threatened, I will forever appreciate the fact that I am alive and healthy—that's the positive. But now even though it is my chosen career to talk about breast cancer, there are some days that go by in which I honestly forget to include myself as someone who has had the disease. That never happened before my reconstruction. Of course there were other benefits to this surgery as well. I can wear just about anything I like and I no longer feel lopsided when my bra comes off. For me, breast reconstruction was the right choice. For you, it may not be.

If you are considering this surgery for yourself, you need to know what it entails. There are two major types of reconstructive surgery: immediate— at the time of mastectomy—and delayed—performed months or years after the mastectomy. *Talk to your surgeon about it before your mastectomy, if possible*, because he might tell you that you are a candidate for immediate reconstruction or if not, the position of the mastectomy incision may affect the later reconstruction procedure.

If you have already had a mastectomy and are just now considering the option of reconstruction, don't worry. Almost every breast cancer patient is a candidate for reconstruction. Scarred, radiation-damaged, grafted, thin, or tight skin, and even the absence of chest muscles are no longer obstacles to successful reconstruction.

Talking to other women who have gone through the surgery will help you get a new perspective if you are unsure about the procedure. Try to find women of approximately your own age to talk with, as their questions and thoughts may be similar to yours. If you can't find any, call the American Cancer Society's "Reach to Recovery" program (see Resources, page 192).

Choosing a Reconstructive Surgeon

The most important factor in choosing a reconstructive surgeon is finding someone who is experienced, and technically and medically competent. It is also important to find a physician who is thoughtful and understanding of the psychological impact breast surgery of any kind has on a woman. Your oncologist and/or surgeon may be helpful in giving you some names of reconstructive surgeons to interview. Or consult the American Society of Plastic and Reconstructive Surgeons (see Resources, page 189).

When talking with the surgeon, discuss your feelings about the procedure openly and candidly. This will help you to decide if you are comfortable talking to him or her and able to establish the necessary rapport. Ask to see photographs of the surgeon's work and get the names and phone numbers of some of his or her other patients.

Here is a list of questions that may help you get started in your interviewing process. You will probably have many more to add to this list. As always, you should continue to ask questions until the procedure is clear in your mind.

1. What type of reconstructive surgery do you recommend for me, and why?
2. What kind of implant are you suggesting, and why?
3. What are the risks and benefits associated with this type of surgery?
4. How much experience have you had with this type of surgery?
5. May I see photographs of other patients who have had the various types of reconstruction?
6. May I speak with other patients about the procedure?
7. What can I expect my reconstructed breast to look and feel like after surgery? How, if at all, will this change in six months or a year?
8. How long will I be in the hospital?
9. How long is the recovery period following surgery?
10. What should I do or avoid doing to ensure a safe and fast recovery?
11. How soon can I have this operation?
12. What else should I consider before committing to reconstructive surgery?
13. What about my other breast?
14. How do you get mammograms after reconstruction?
15. How much will it cost? Will this operation be covered by my insurance?

When Should Reconstruction Be Performed?

You should know that there is still a debate going on as to how soon a woman should have reconstruction following her mastectomy. Some doctors feel that in certain situations, when the malignant tumor is very small and noninvasive, it is perfectly safe to have reconstruction during the same surgical procedure as the mastectomy. Some doctors feel that even if the tumor is large, reconstructive surgery can be done at the same time as the mastectomy without affecting the ultimate prognosis one way or the other. However, there are many doctors who disagree with this theory completely. They feel that delaying reconstruction to determine lymph node involvement is in the patient's best interest. Some surgeons and oncologists feel that if a recurrence is going to happen, it is likely to occur within two years following the mastectomy. While most doctors will agree that breast reconstruction does not interfere with the detection of recurrent cancer, some feel that having to remove the implant in order to treat a recurrence is an unnecessary inconvenience for the patient. There are still other surgeons who feel that even if all the prognostic features of a cancer are good, meaning the tumor is small, noninvasive, and nonaggressive, it is best to wait a minimum of six months because this delay will improve the blood supply to the area, which will result in better healing and a prettier cosmetic result. To determine what is appropriate for you, I suggest you discuss all the variables with your oncologist, your breast surgeon, and the reconstructive surgeon you have chosen. Together you should be able to come up with a plan that fits both your personal needs and your medical needs.

Types of Reconstructive Surgery

Reconstruction of the entire breast, including the nipple and areola, will take at least two operations. Most doctors prefer to delay adding the nipple and areola to allow the new breast tissue to settle in. If adjustments need to be made on the implant, they can be done at the time the nipple and areola are added. If your primary reason for wanting reconstruction is just to have the freedom of dressing you lose by wearing a prosthesis, you may choose to forgo adding the nipple and areola at all. This is not uncommon.

There are three common procedures used in breast reconstruction. As in all types of breast cancer treatment, each woman's case is individual and the procedure that is the best for you should be discussed thoroughly before a final decision is made.

Simple Breast Reconstruction

This procedure is done when the patient has a healthy chest muscle and enough good-quality skin to cover the implant. The quality of skin is determined by its thickness and its aesthetic appearance. During this procedure, the surgeon makes a small incision along the lower portion of the breast area, either by reopening the original mastectomy scar or by making a new incision. The implant is then inserted in a pocket created under the chest muscle. The implants are strong silicone rubber sacs filled with silicone gel and other fluids that come in a variety of shapes and sizes in order to match the other breast as well as possible. (Now, one of the most commonly used implants has a coating or covering that helps keep scar tissue from binding to it and hardening. This helps keep the breast more soft and supple.) A drain will be inserted to remove the fluid that may accumulate during the next few days in the area of the "new" breast. The incision is then closed. The entire operation takes approximately two hours to be completed, and then the patient is sent home.

Occasionally, although the skin over the chest is aesthetically appealing, it is too tight to handle the implant comfortably. In this case, a doctor may insert a *tissue expander*, which is nothing more than a deflated implant. At the time of insertion the implant is flat, but it contains a valve through which fluid can be added. Each week the surgeon will inflate the implant a little by adding a little more fluid, giving the skin time to stretch slowly. When the implant reaches the size that best matches the other breast, it is removed and a permanent implant is inserted in its place.

Latissimus Dorsi Reconstruction

This procedure is done when more radical surgery has removed some or all of the chest muscles and a large amount of skin so that there is not enough soft tissue to cover the implant. During this operation, the surgeon transfers skin and muscle from the back to the site of the mastectomy. In order to create a new muscle on the front of the chest, the surgeon uses the large flat muscle on the back called the latissimus dorsi. An implant is then inserted beneath the "new" chest muscle. Drains are inserted to remove the fluid around the site and left in place for about three days. In addition to the mastectomy scar on the chest, the patient will now also have a scar on her back. The recovery time is longer because of the two incisions.

Rectus Abdominus Reconstruction

This procedure is also used on women whose mastectomy has removed too much muscle and skin to effectively hold an implant in place naturally. To create a chest muscle, the surgeon will transfer one of the two abdominal muscles, technically called the rectus abdominus muscles, from the stomach to the chest. This flap of muscle, skin, and fat is shaped into the contour of the opposite breast. If there is enough abdominal tissue available, no implant is needed. This procedure also tightens the abdominal muscles, giving a woman a "tummy tuck" at the same time as her reconstruction. The patient will have a scar across the lower abdomen in addition to the mastectomy scar on her chest. Because there are, in effect, two surgeries being done simultaneously, recovery may be prolonged.

The following slides show the chronology of Latissimus Dorsi reconstruction, the transfer of skin and muscle from the back to the site of the mastectomy. (PHOTOS TAKEN BY TERRY GENTRY, COURTESY OF DR. FRITZ BARTON)

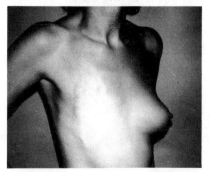

(23) Patient following modified radical mastectomy.

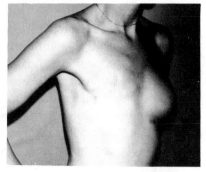

(24) Four months later. Notice how the scar has diminished.

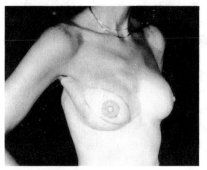

(25) Four months later, after the reconstruction.

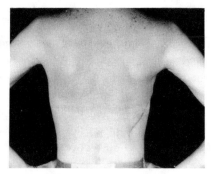

(26) Back view, taken at the same time. The scar shows the area of the graft.

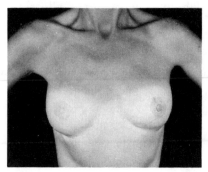

(27) Five years later, front view and

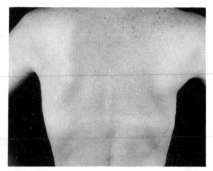

(28) back view.

The following slides show the chronology of Rectus Abdominus reconstruction, the transfer of an abdominal muscle from the stomach to the chest.

TAKEN BY TERRY GENTRY, COURTESY OF DR. FRITZ BARTON)

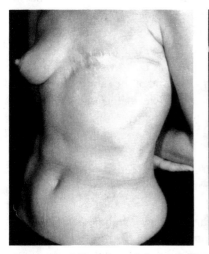

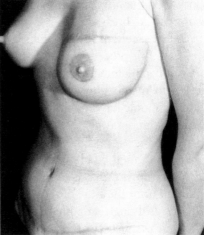

(29) Patient following modified radical mastectomy.

(30) One year later, patient following the reconstruction.

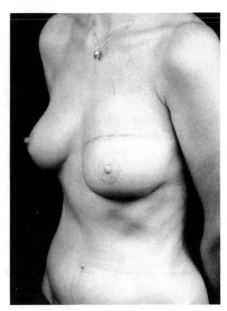

(31) One year later.

Nipple Reconstruction

There are several different ways a nipple can be created for the reconstructed breast. If a woman has large nipples, one option may be to borrow a portion of the nipple from the normal breast and have it transferred to the reconstructed breast. This is a good choice, when possible, because it ensures an excellent color match. Unfortunately, not all women have large nipples so this procedure is not always an option. If a woman's nipple has a naturally pink tone, the surgeon can graft some of the skin located behind her ear to match the skin of the normal nipple to the new nipple. If a woman's nipple has a naturally brown tone, the surgeon may graft some of the skin from her inner thigh or vaginal lips in an attempt to achieve a good match.

One other method of nipple reconstruction is to remove the nipple from the breast during mastectomy and temporarily attach it to the thigh or abdomen until the time of reconstruction. This procedure is called *nipple banking*. Although it does ensure a nearly perfect match in size and color, many doctors feel it carries an element of danger. If there are malignant cancer cells on the nipple, nipple banking will transplant those cancer cells back onto the reconstructed breast.

In Summary

For some women, breast reconstruction has a profoundly positive psychological impact. For other women, it is an unnecessary extravagance. And then there is the consideration that it is a major operation requiring general anesthesia. The decision is one that requires a lot of research and discussion. Whether you choose one of these procedures or not, it is important that you know they exist. A major part of being a strong, aggressive cancer patient is understanding all of your options.

CHAPTER EIGHT

Appearance and Recovery

> Do wear make-up—it's so vain not to.
>
> —COCO CHANEL

*T*here is probably no other time in a woman's life when she feels less like making herself look attractive than while she is being treated for cancer, yet I know of no other time when the effort is more rewarding. That effort includes paying attention to your makeup and wardrobe, and exercising to keep your body attractive, too.

I have seen and spoken to many breast cancer patients over the past twelve years. Some of the women I have spoken to have had early-stage breast cancer, others have been more advanced. I have noticed a certain pattern in the women who have had success in their treatment. They seem to be a little more vain, a bit more concerned about self-image, and a little more willing to do whatever it takes to preserve that image than the women who weren't as successful.

But beauty is more than the way you look. It is also the way you view life. A woman who always sees the bright side is often considered more beautiful than her negative counterpart, regardless of what she actually looks like. This is not to say that one should "view the world through rose-colored glasses." The ability to see things exactly the way they are and yet find the best in even the worst situation is indeed a gift—*one that can and should be cultivated.*

Still, almost everyone will agree that when you look good, you feel better. I know several women who have been in the depths of cancer despair and no one would ever have known it to look at them. Mary Tullie Critcher, a board member of the Komen Foundation and a cancer patient, is one of those women. I distinctly remember her coming to a meeting immediately following a chemotherapy treatment. Most women in her condition would not have shown up for the meeting at all. But Mary Tullie was there, looking more beautiful and more pulled together than ever before. She was wearing a soft, silky scarf on her head over which she wore a wonderful hat that matched her dress. The look was quite chic. Mary Tullie is a typical American wife and mother. What inspired her to make such a noble effort? "My family was very upset and frightened by my illness," Mary Tullie explained. "When they saw me looking as if I felt good, they believed I was getting better. The doctors and nurses at the Medical Center also seemed to get a lift when I showed up for a check-up or a treatment looking well. Other patients, too, took note of my scarves and hats, wanting to know where they came from or how I did it. Pretty soon, if even for just a short while, I forgot how sick I was."

Another very special woman is the late GiGi Hill. GiGi was given less than a 5 percent chance of living five years after being diagnosed with metastatic breast cancer in 1980. Knowing exactly what the odds were, GiGi made up her mind that she was going to live those five years with style and grace. She never missed a charity event, never missed a party, was always there for her family and friends, and always looked divine. She took the time to see that her makeup was applied beautifully and that her wigs were always in place. In October of 1985, GiGi was given the Betty Ford Award at the Komen Awards Luncheon. She marched up on that stage in front of some 1500 people, shook Mrs. Ford's hand, and flashed her most gorgeous smile. The audience went wild. No one could have guessed from her appearance that she was only days away from death.

Taking the time to make yourself look as good as possible will help you get through your illness. When you look sick, people are bound to inquire about it—that's human nature. If everyone you meet asks you what's wrong, *it will be difficult to get past your illness and get on with your life.*

Taking the time to make yourself look as good as possible will also do wonders for your morale. I guarantee it. There are all kinds of uncomplicated tricks you can use to make the process easier and more successful. Several of them I learned through my own experimentation. Some I picked up from other cancer patients, and still others I found out about through the "Look Good . . . Feel Better" program (see Resources, page 185) and from a book titled *Beauty and Cancer* (Resources, page 185). They worked for me; I hope they'll work for you.

Hair

The most traumatic aesthetic side effect of cancer treatment is, of course, the loss of hair (alopecia). Your hair surrounds your most prominent means of communication, your face—no wonder it is so important. For most women, the possibility of going around without hair is unthinkable. Scars from surgery can be concealed without anyone knowing about them. Covering a bald head is more difficult. I found the wigs that look the most natural to be the most time-consuming and difficult to put on. Wearing the obviously fake hair was hassle free, but I had to realize that strangers would know I was sick. It didn't matter—I wanted to get on with my life. The good news is, hair loss due to chemotherapy is almost always temporary. In the meantime, you can hide your loss by wearing wigs, scarves, and hats. Use the time to experiment with different styles and/or colors. Making the most of this emotional trauma will do wonders for your morale.

Wigs

One of the most natural-looking wigs is made in Italy from "virgin" hair. Virgin hair is hair that has never been chemically treated (permed or colored). These wigs range in price from $45 to $2000, depending on how they are made. Synthetic wigs are usually less expensive and much easier to take care of. I have seen great improvement in the synthetic wigs today compared to the time when I was being treated.

In choosing a wig for yourself, try to go to a person who specializes in or has a keen understanding of women with cancer. This is a very emotional and vulnerable time for any woman and the last thing you need is an insensitive sales clerk pushing a product that is simply not you. Make sure that wherever you go has a place you can be helped in private. Sometimes an owner will open the salon at "off" hours to ensure your privacy, or if you are really lucky, you may find someone who will come to your home.

Obviously, what you are striving for is to look as normal as possible. I cut my hair short before I started with the chemotherapy so the change would not seem as drastic to me. Many women find it easier to make the adjustment from short hair to no hair rather than from long hair to no hair. It is difficult to get a true fit for a wig until you have lost all your hair, although you may want to have the process organized and ready before that time. If you choose a wig before you've lost your hair, ask if you can leave a deposit and pay for the wig later when you are sure the fit will be correct. If you opt to wait until you can ensure the perfect fit, bring with you a couple of photographs with your hair looking just the way you like it. That way, the specialist can do his or her best to make you look as close as possible to the way you are used to seeing yourself .

The concern of every woman who purchases a wig, regardless of the reason, is that it will stay in place. We can all imagine the humiliation of the first gust of wind that comes along and leaves us standing in the middle of a crowd bald-headed and mortified. I found that using the foot of a pair of nylons as a cap over my head before applying the wig helped to keep it firmly in place. I also used a light-weight double-sided tape around the edges of my wig to ensure a snug fit.

Today, I am told, suction is the newest and most reliable way to keep a wig safely in its place. The hairs are implanted to a customized plastic mold made of your head which is used as the base of the wig. The fit is comfortable, and you can move around as freely as if the hair were all your own.

A note about insurance: Although every insurance company has its own rules and regulations about what is and isn't covered, most consider the loss of hair as they would the loss of a limb requiring a prosthesis. Have your physician write out a prescription for a "wig prosthesis" and make sure your wig salon uses the word *prosthesis* on the sales receipt so that it is not confused with a wig purchased for cosmetic reasons. Consult the Health Insurance Association of America (see Resources, page 190).

Scarves and Hats

Scarves are a terrific alternative to wigs. They are fast, simple, and stylish. You can purchase scarves in a variety of different textures and colors to complement any outfit. They should be cotton rather than silk or polyester as these materials have a tendency to slip around on the head. The best size to use is either a 26-inch or a 28-inch square. There are dozens of different ways to tie scarves into interesting headwraps, ranging from very conservative to very avant-garde. The important thing is to develop a style you are comfortable with. Many times, the look is so fabulous, women keep right on wearing scarves long after their hair returns.

Hats can be an equally charming touch to complete an outfit. Most hats don't cover the entire head, however, so it is important to wear them over a scarf. Berets and caps will give you a sporty, fun look; fedoras a more classic, conservative look; and wide-brimmed hats will protect your skin, which will be extra sensitive at this time, from the sun and wind.

Skin

Any authority on beauty will tell you repeatedly that even the strongest, thickest skin should be treated delicately. Skin that is being subjected to radiation and/or chemotherapy can be especially tender and sensitive. Be gentle. When washing your face, use a liquid or cream cleanser; they are less harsh than soap. Even if your skin is oily, it is still extra-vulnerable right now. Look for an oil-free cleanser and then follow up with an astringent or whatever your regular routine involves.

Some women find that while going through radiation and chemotherapy, their skin is dry, even when normally it is on the oilier side. Moisturizers, skin lotions, and body oils will take away the dry, irritated, chapped feeling caused by your treatments. Occasionally, the skin will react to the fragrance in some of these products. If this should happen to you, don't despair—you will not have to give them up. Almost every major cosmetic and toiletry company makes a line of products that is fragrance-free.

Because your skin is so sensitive, take your baths and showers in water that is warm rather than hot, especially if you are receiving radiation. The radiation may already be causing your skin to appear red and irritated. Submerging your body in hot water may make it worse.

If you are experiencing hair loss from chemotherapy, be sure not to neglect your scalp just because there may be little or no hair on your head. If you suffered with the problems of dryness, itching, and dandruff before your hair loss, you will suffer with them during and after your hair loss as well. It is thought that a daily massaging will stimulate blood flow in the area and may produce a stronger, healthier, and shinier head of hair after chemotherapy.

Sun

By now we have all heard about the damage too much sun can do to the skin. Despite the warnings of skin cancer and premature aging, however, many women still find it necessary to spend countless hours in the sun during the summer and never miss a day in the tanning booth during the winter.

It is especially important while you are undergoing cancer treatment to be careful of sun exposure. Too much sun while taking such chemotherapy drugs as actinomycin D, bleomycin sulfate, dacarbazine, doxorubicin hydrochloride (Adriamycin), Fluorouracil (5-FU), methotrexate, and vinblastine sulfate (Velban) can cause permanent changes in the skin pigment.

Still, having a "healthy glow" will be the first thing you, your family, and your friends will look for as proof that you are well on your way to recovery. Using a sunscreen of SPF (sun protection factor) 15 or higher will keep you safe from the sun's harmful rays (if applied faithfully every two hours and after swimming) and still allow a slow tan. If you want to look healthy but refuse to submit your skin to potential sun damage, don't forget the wonders of makeup.

Makeup

Carefully applied makeup can be very helpful at this time. For some women experimenting with cosmetics is fun, and trying to make yourself look healthy at this time presents an interesting challenge. Even if you have always detested wearing cosmetics, you might want to give them a try. Maybe you've thought the look was unnatural or perhaps you've never wanted to take the time and trouble. You are not alone. Many women prefer a more natural look and feel to their skin. But now, while you are experiencing some of the side effects of breast cancer treatment, the "natural look" may not be the most flattering. Temporary changes in skin color can make you appear yellow, gray, washed-out, pale, or in some cases, flushed and ruddy. You may be experiencing puffiness and either complete or partial loss of eyebrows and eyelashes. A little bit of knowledge on just the basics of makeup artistry can give you the lift you need. Most of the aesthetic side effects of chemotherapy and radiation can be corrected with cosmetics.

Changes in skin color can be corrected with such products as foundation and under-eye concealer. If your skin has turned gray or yellowish, wear a foundation with a rose or pink hue. On the other hand, if you are experiencing a ruddy, red tone in your complexion, wear a foundation with a peachy hue. This will counterbalance the temporary color change. Dark circles under the eyes can be virtually eliminated with under-eye concealer. There are many different formulas of this product with many different consistencies.

If your eyebrows have fallen out, either completely or partially, don't use eyebrow pencil to fill them in. Eyebrow pencil has a tendency to look harsh and phony. Using a powder eyebrow color allows you to recreate the look of eyebrows in a much softer, gentler manner.

Every woman wants to have long, lustrous eyelashes; chemotherapy can take that dream away for a little while. Wearing false eyelashes can help recreate the look. I found, as have many cancer patients and noncancer patients alike, that the individual lashes are far more natural-looking than the strip lashes. Once you get the hang of it, these individual lashes are a cinch to apply. You can wear them by themselves or to supplement any existing lashes. And if you use a good glue, they can stay in place for weeks, looking fabulous.

These are actually only a few of the many tricks cosmetics can do for you at this special time in your life. If you are not comfortable playing with the products, treat yourself to a makeover. At a local department store, there is usually no charge for a cosmetic makeover, but in most cases, there is little or no privacy. If you go to a private salon, the cost will be anywhere from $40 to $200, but you will be helped by a licensed cosmetician who may be more familiar with your particular needs. Even if you are an expert at makeup application, it is sometimes fun to see what someone else might do with your face.

Remember that seeing you look good is equally important to your friends and family as it is to you—sometimes more so. Do make an effort to look your best, even if it's just a little lip gloss and blusher—for their sake.

Dressing

The two most common treatments for women with breast cancer that affect clothing are the mastectomy and the insertion of a subclavian catheter. Also, of course, there is a short time after a lumpectomy and/or biopsy that you might feel a little sore or uncomfortable, but that should pass within a week or two.

The good news is that today a woman can dress very casually and comfortably and still be considered chic and fashionable. At one time, sweat suits were worn only in the gym, but now they can be worn almost anywhere. Even with dressier clothes, more attention is paid to comfort now than ever before.

When dressing immediately after surgery or to cover a venous access device, try to wear blouses that are loose-fitting. The catheter sits right below the clavicle (collarbone) and halfway between the neck and shoulder. Big, soft collars will cover the area without causing any discomfort. Scarves strategically thrown over the shoulder will also help camouflage the catheter. Shoulder pads lift the fabric away from the body, keeping the area free from abrasion.

Breast Prostheses

If you have had a mastectomy, you will need to wear a breast prosthesis, which is an artificial device replacing your breast. Besides the obvious advantage of making the body look "normal," the prosthesis will keep your body weight balanced. Without the prosthesis in place, your upper body will be lopsided, which could cause a great deal of discomfort in your back, shoulders, and neck. Today, breast prostheses have been revamped for the active woman. They can be worn doing almost anything, even swimming. And, they can be worn with just about any type of outfit except, of course, one that shows cleavage.

There are several different types of breast forms to choose from. Some feel quite rubbery and heavy; others very airy. The materials vary significantly from prosthesis to prosthesis. They may be filled with water, air, gel, polyurethane foam, or foam rubber. The kind you will find most comfortable will be based on your bra size, cup size, and the actual shape and weight of your other breast.

At night, many women wear a sleep form to bed because the back, neck, and shoulders are susceptible to the same strain lying down as they are standing up and moving around. The sleep forms are not as heavy as the silicone forms worn during the day. They are usually made of polyester, cotton, or foam.

Your emotional recovery walks hand in hand with your personal self-image. Your comfort plays a large role in how you feel and the speediness of your ability to get back into the mainstream. For this reason, it is imperative that in being fitted for your prosthesis you seek the advice of a qualified expert. Look in the yellow pages under brassieres or contact the local chapter of the American Cancer Society's "Reach to Recovery" program (see Resources, page 192) or the Susan G. Komen Breast Cancer Foundation (page 192) for more information.

Exercise

There is no question that a mastectomy is major surgery. Besides making you feel lopsided there is a great deal of discomfort and stiffness involved. Fortunately, having a mastectomy rarely causes any permanent limitations in movement and often, steady exercise can speed up your recovery. However, women who have lost their chest muscles through a radical mastectomy (very uncommon today) may not regain 100 percent of their original strength in the affected arm and shoulder. Still, a regular exercise routine can alleviate some of the tightness in the chest.

Exercise, as was proven in my case, is also very helpful in relieving the symptoms of lymphedema, which is the swelling of the arm following the removal of the lymph nodes in the armpit (axilla).

No exercise program should be contemplated or begun without the expressed consent and guidance of your surgeon. Immediately following your surgery, while you are still in the hospital, a physical therapist will come to your room and gently lift and rotate your shoulder. The therapist may also teach you some deep-breathing exercises to expand the chest cavity, reduce muscle tension, and increase tolerance for pain. In the beginning, you should refrain from doing such "strenuous activities" as brushing your hair or reaching for the telephone with the affected arm. Raising the arm over the head is not recommended until approximately seven days following your surgery.

As soon as your doctor gives you the go-ahead, a low-key exercise regime should be your next physical goal. The exercises that follow have been approved by the National Cancer Institute and are taken directly from *The Breast Cancer Digest* (see Resources, page 177). They are very mild and are not meant to do anything but relieve stiffness. You can do them in your nightgown, if you choose. Be gentle with yourself—this is not "Go for the burn"! Still, no exercise should be done without a discussion with your doctor.

- Lie on your back in bed with your arms at your side. Raise your right arm straight up and back, trying to touch the headboard. Do this 10 times. Repeat with left arm.
- Either sitting or standing, raise your shoulders. Rotate them forward, down, and back in a circular motion to loosen your chest, shoulders, and upper back muscles. Do this 30 times.
- Lying on your back in bed, clasp your hands behind your head and push your elbows into the mattress. Do this 10 times.
- Start with your arms at your sides. Keeping your upper arms at your sides and bending your elbows, raise your lower arms to a position at a 90 degree angle from your body, with your palms facing up. Curl your hands into fists. Rotating your shoulders and simultaneously

twisting your wrists forward, "flip" your forearms over so that the backs of your hands and the upper side of your forearms are on top. Your forearms will feel some pressure. Do this 20 times.

- Either sitting or standing, elevate your arm and clench and unclench your fist. Do this 20 times with your left arm and 20 times with your right arm.

- Either lying flat on your back or standing up straight, inhale and exhale deeply. Do this 20 times.

- Either sitting or standing, slowly turn your head so that your chin is pointing first left and then right. Cock your head sideways in each direction. Do this 20 times.

The key is to exercise only to the point where it begins to feel uncomfortable—don't push yourself. Remember, regular exercise will speed your physical recovery, which will enhance your appearance and benefit your emotional recovery.

Emotional Recovery

To all of the tips above on prostheses, wigs, makeup, clothing, and exercise, one more must be added. There's a risk factor in your emotional recovery: depression. Depression is anger turned inward. Depression, if it strikes, can cause you to say, "Why bother taking care of myself." The good news is that there are people who can help you overcome this problem, too. See Resources, Reach to Recovery, page 192; Y-Me, page 188; and Regional Support Organizations, page 195.

CHAPTER NINE

Sexuality

> *Some people are still unaware that reality contains unparalleled beauties. The fantastic and unexpected, the ever-changing and renewing is nowhere so exemplified as in real life itself.*
>
> *—BERENICE ABBOTT*

Self-image, as it pertains to sexuality, can be a monumental issue for any woman. It is ingrained in our psyches at an early age through movies, television, books, and magazines that in order to be attractive and desirable to men, we have to have a certain *look.* Flat stomachs, shapely hips, lean legs, and full breasts are the components of a "sexy"-looking woman, so they say. This kind of pressure, we all know, is unhealthy and unfair. Men, of course, do not have a specific physical "standard of excellence" to live up to, in order to be considered attractive and desirable.

A woman who has been diagnosed with breast cancer faces three major losses with which she must come to terms. The first is loss of life. The stage of her disease, her spirit and willingness to fight, and her body's ability to *work with* the prescribed treatment are all factors that will determine her prognosis. The second is the loss of her breast. Some women fear the loss of a breast will make them less than whole, that their altered body will prevent them from ever having a normal life again or keep them from being a complete woman. The third loss is the loss of her hair. Because 99 percent of the time hair loss is only temporary, a woman's fear of it is often dismissed without a lot of psychological evaluation. But I can tell you, through personal experience and through talking with literally thousands of cancer patients, that this fear is a real one for a woman's hair has a significant effect on her ability to feel desirable.

Some women are so preoccupied with the thought of losing their sexuality that they will opt to forgo what could be life-saving surgery altogether. My sister Suzy is a prime example. On the day my breast cancer was diagnosed, my ultimate concern was to save my life, to get rid of the cancer as thoroughly and as quickly as possible. This was based on my fear of going through the same slow, painful death as Suzy did and the fact that I was an educated cancer patient. My priorities were pre-established. Every time I had gone in for a biopsy prior to then, I had thought long and hard about what I would do if the tumor was malignant. Still, on that evening before my surgery at M.D. Anderson, sitting in the bed looking at Norman, I quietly wondered how he would relate to his relatively new wife's coming home without a breast. My wonderful friend Sharon McCutchin called me on the telephone and, sensing my concern, said in her long Texas drawl, "Honey, don't worry about it. *That's* not what they really care about, anyway." All I could do was pray she was right.

In the two years that passed between my mastectomy and my reconstruction, I learned a great deal about the true meaning of sexuality. Once again, what works for one woman may not work for another, but I want to share this with you, with the hope of reaching anyone who can possibly benefit from my experience.

I learned that my ability to be desirable to Norman had little to do with my breasts (or lack thereof). I learned that a kind smile, a gentle touch, and a sweet conversation did more for our romance than sexy lingerie. From the day we met we had always been able to communicate. If we were going to get through this without losing the sparkle, we had to continue to talk openly and honestly about the situation. The truth is that after my surgery and the treatment that followed, quite often I wasn't in the mood for romance. It was up to me to make sure that this was not misinterpreted as a lack of love. Norman, being the kind of man he is, understood my feelings. I made it a point to let him know how much I loved him and needed him and to show him that I was trying to get well. Whenever I could help it, and sometimes I couldn't, I tried desperately not to feel sorry for myself and to maintain a cheery disposition. Norman often expressed his pride in my fight to beat the disease. This encouragement "egged me on" and gave me the incentive to keep trying even on those days when I wanted to give up. His lack of pressure and expectations of me on a sexual level made me try harder to please him.

The fact of the matter is that a mastectomy rarely affects the man's pleasure or ability to be fulfilled sexually. It is the woman's loss of a sensitive, sexual area that may affect *her* sense of pleasure. There is no reason why, after a few initial adjustments, a couple cannot rekindle a romance that is equally as sensual and full of love as it was before her surgery. Sometimes, when two people acknowledge their own mortality, as a run-in with cancer often forces them to do, their newfound appreciation for life will bring them closer than ever before.

I think it is vitally important for all women before, during, and after breast cancer to take the time to re-evaluate what it means to be a "total woman." Is it the size and shape of our breasts and how we look in a bathing suit? Or is it our ability to nurture and protect those we love? I have for a long time felt that women have a sixth sense, if you will, which encompasses a capability to give open and unconditional love in a deeper more passionate manner than men will ever have. It is, I think, ingrained in women, a gift we were given naturally—something we have no control over. It is this compassion from which true sexuality is born. Of course, we all want to be thought of as attractive and desirable. But on what is this desirability based? Certainly not on our ability to fill a bra. If we do what we need to do in order to be and feel healthy—eat right and exercise—we will have the energy it takes to tackle life with spirit and grace. To me, *that's* what makes a woman sensual. Looking good is usually an added benefit that comes along with doing what it takes to feel good.

Sometimes, however, eating right and exercising aren't enough to maintain a healthy body. Breast cancer chooses its victims for no apparent rhyme or reason. The healthiest woman in the world can get breast cancer. When this happens she has new choices to make. And sometimes, one of those choices will be to have a mastectomy. If she can get herself in a mindset to believe that her energy and spirit for living are what make her sexy, she will be much better equipped to handle the emotional and psychological stress involved in losing a breast.

The sexual problems some couples face after a lumpectomy or mastectomy are often the result of preconceived notions on the part of either partner. For example, the man is often afraid to touch the woman after surgery for fear that she may not be up to it or that he may hurt her accidentally in the process. The woman, who has probably already thought herself no longer desirable, may take his lack of overtures as the justification of her feelings. She then will be reluctant to initiate a sexual encounter out of fear of further rejection. This is a very common situation and one that can escalate way out of proportion without open and honest communication. As uncomfortable as it may be at first, it is in a couple's best interest to resume sexual activity, even on the mildest scale, as soon as physically possible. If you have tried and just can't seem to muster up the desire for sex after your surgery, or you cannot get a feeling of desire from your partner, you both might want to consider seeing a sex therapist to open the lines of communication.

But what about the single woman who goes through the mastectomy without a husband or boyfriend? What happens when her surgery is complete and she feels like "getting out there" again in the dating circle? When you go through the diagnosis and treatment with a partner, regardless of the difficulties that may ensue, at least you don't have to carry the burden of a very private and personal secret a woman without a partner holds inside her waiting for the appropriate time to divulge. When *is* the appropriate time to tell a man you are dating that you've had a mastectomy? Obviously, for every couple the situation will be different. Some women like to get it out in the open at the very beginning of a relationship. Others prefer to wait and see if the relationship will progress enough to become intimate at all.

The late Sherri Firnberg, a darling young woman actively involved in the Komen Foundation, was at age twenty-eight bravely and optimistically beginning treatment for her second recurrence. Sherri was not married, and every time she met a new man, she went through the dilemma of when to tell him. She said, "My first choice is really to keep it a secret. It's not that I have a problem talking about the experience—I don't. But I like to let people see that I'm okay before I start to talk about the cancer. Some people react funny when they hear the word. All of a sudden, they look at you as if you are going to fall apart right in front of them. Unfortunately, though, my secret isn't often a secret for very long. Inevitably, my date and I will run into someone I know and they'll ask how I'm doing. At that point I feel sort of obligated to tell. I did meet a man I thought was special. He turned out not to be, but when we first met, we hit it off right away and I immediately felt close to him. I ran over to his house and told him everything. I was relieved when he said it didn't bother him at all. This man was a little older than most of the men I have dated. Maybe it isn't fair to make such a generalization, but so far I have found that older men take the news much better than younger men."

It is important to handle this in a manner that makes you feel comfortable. While constantly talking about it may not be the best way to put the past behind you, your breast cancer and subsequent mastectomy are certainly nothing to be ashamed of. When the situation calls for it, speaking from your heart about your experience can help bring you close to friends in general and perhaps add an element of intimacy and closeness to conversations with potential lovers. With the threat of AIDS on everyone's mind these days, we are seeing an overall slowdown in sexual activity. People are taking the time, once again, to get to know each other before adding the sexual dimension to their relationships. I can't help but feel this is a good thing for all couples, but for women who are trying to decide who should know about their medical past, it is especially helpful.

Whether you are happily married, unhappily married, divorced, separated, widowed, or single, one thing is for sure: If you would like to begin or continue a successful sexual relationship, you must first be comfortable with your own self-image. Nobody can give that to you—it must come from within. Remember that dealing with a mastectomy isn't easy for anyone. Your friends, lovers, and children will take their cue from you. If you honestly believe that you are every bit the woman you were before your surgery, so will all who know you and come to know you. And perhaps, if you are lucky, you will find, just as I did, that developing the inner strength to take on cancer as an opponent gives you a sense of femininity you never knew existed. Once you learn that *real* sensuality comes from within the heart and soul, you will also learn that it can never be taken away.

CHAPTER TEN

*Talk happiness.
The world is sad
enough without
your woe.*

—*ELLA WHEELER
WILCOX*

Talking About Your Breast Cancer

As I have mentioned earlier, talking about breast cancer can be difficult. Many people have not been brought up to discuss intimate topics with others comfortably. I know in my heart that in the beginning my own husband was not completely at ease with the subject. The intimacy of this disease, coupled with the fear of cancer in general, often creates a communication block within the family, among friends, and at the workplace. The stage of your cancer, combined with your prescribed treatment and how your disease responds to that treatment, will determine the kinds of challenges you are forced to meet along the way.

When and how much to tell your friends, family, and business associates are factors to be considered carefully. As a rule, I feel that honesty is, as always, the best policy. However, you will know, better than anyone else, in whom you can confide.

Having breast cancer is nothing to be embarrassed about. Being surrounded by a close support group will make the ordeal easier and less stressful. You must be prepared, though, for those who react in an unexpected manner. There are people who are still so afraid of the word *cancer* that they can't bring themselves to talk about it. This can be especially difficult. Friends, family, and business associates with whom you have always been able to communicate easily may now seem to withdraw just at the time when you need them the most. People who don't understand cancer and how its treatment works are often so afraid of *saying the wrong thing*, they may say nothing at all. You may find this very hurtful. Be patient. Those who love and care about you will also feel like victims of your disease. Their terror and anger over what has happened can manifest itself in "funny" ways.

Most people will take their lead from you. If you learn to talk honestly, openly, and optimistically about your breast cancer, they will too. Fair or not, don't be surprised to discover that just when you need to be comforted and nurtured more than at any other time in your life, *you* are the one doing much of the comforting and nurturing. That, my friends, goes with the territory of being a woman.

You can help people by telling them you know they care and you *do* want to talk about it, or you can say, "I know you care and that you have questions, but I don't want to discuss it today." For many families, the trauma of dealing with a life-threatening disease brings them closer than ever before. My friend Chris Plunkett, a wife and mother of four older sons and a fifteen-year-old daughter, Sarah, has breast cancer which has turned into metastatic disease. She has been and continues to be a woman of amazing strength. Chris has explained to her family exactly what is happening and they, as a group, are involved in all her treatment decisions. Young Sarah has proven to be her mother's greatest inspiration. This little girl wants more than anything to have her mother there for her as she goes through her teen-age years and on into adulthood. Sarah has educated herself about breast cancer and is quite knowledgeable about all aspects of the disease. She volunteers her time to the Komen Foundation, speaking to groups of all ages about what the family can do to support a mother with breast cancer. When Sarah Plunkett addresses an audience, there isn't a dry eye in the house.

Another friend, Gretchen Poston, handled her situation very differently. When Gretchen was diagnosed with breast cancer, she told no one. She went through surgery and chemotherapy all by herself. On the days when the treatment was difficult to endure, she said she wasn't feeling well and stayed at home. She cut her hair short before her chemotherapy began and wore a well-made wig when her hair fell out. Afterward, when Gretchen felt up to it, she did talk about the experience. Her friends were puzzled that she hadn't taken them into her confidence. Gretchen explained that it wasn't a matter of not trusting her friends, it was just that she felt she could get through the ordeal more successfully without the pity of others. As she did. As in all matters concerning breast cancer, this too is a personal decision. I know that I could not have fought the disease as strongly as I did without the love and support of my friends. But there are certain times and situations in a woman's life when she may be on her own. This does not mean she can't survive the disease; there is always someone to talk to. An extensive list of support groups appears in the Resource section at the back of this book. Another reason my friend Gretchen chose to stay silent was a real concern that some of her clients might feel that she could not carry out her professional responsibilities in her business. Unfortunately, this kind of discrimination does exist. Furthermore, for some women in situations like Gretchen's, pulling the strength and courage to fight from deep inside ultimately gives them a confidence and feeling of self-worth they have never known before.

The women I know who have not only been successful in fighting breast cancer but have been an inspiration to other cancer patients, have known when to discuss their problems and when to keep silent. There is a time and place for both. Remember, there is a difference between developing the ability to talk openly and honestly about the disease and unloading your anger, fear, and confusion onto anyone who happens to cross your path.

CHAPTER ELEVEN

Factors That May Affect the Risk of Breast Cancer

Pray for the dead and fight like hell for the living.

—*MOTHER MARY JONES*

I would like nothing more than to tell you exactly how to prevent breast cancer from entering your life and the lives of those you love. Obviously, I can't do that or I would have used the same preventive measures on myself. What I can tell you is what factors put women at *high risk* of contracting the disease. These factors are to be duly noted and respected but, please, be aware of this: 75 to 80 percent of all women who develop breast cancer *do not* have significant risk factors. Having one or more of what are considered to be known risk factors does not mean you will get breast cancer. Nor does being free of risk factors mean you will not get breast cancer. The bottom line is that we don't yet know how to prevent cancer, but we do know some things that may help decrease your risk.

Known Risk Factors

The most significant risk factors for breast cancer are being a woman and aging.

- The American Cancer Society estimates that of the 175,900 new breast cancer cases diagnosed in 1991, 175,000 will be in women.
- Three fourths of all breast cancers occur in women over thirty-five.
- A woman who has been treated for breast cancer has an increased risk

of developing cancer in the opposite breast. The risk increases depending on family history, age, and type, and on the stage of the original cancer.

- Women with close female relatives (mother, sister, or daughter) who have had breast cancer may be at higher risk than women without the family history. The risk increases if those breast cancers were in both breasts and occurred in more than one generation.

- Women who have had breast biopsies and have had pathologic atypia may be at increased risk of developing breast cancer.

- Although late menopause and early onset of menstruation were once thought to significantly increase breast cancer risk, the risk may be more relative to population rather than to individuals. However, this is still being researched.

Again, these are the known risk factors. (It should also be noted that some women who have more than one close relative with breast cancer may be at increased risk of developing ovarian cancer.) These risk factors should neither frighten you nor give you undue confidence. Any woman can develop breast cancer.

Birth Control Pills

There has been a great deal of press given lately to the correlation between birth control pills and breast cancer. The most reliable scientific information to date finds no consistent link between taking birth control pills and developing breast cancer. Some experts feel that each patient should be carefully examined before a determination is made as to whether she should take birth control pills. If I were taking them, I would be especially diligent about adhering to a regular routine of breast self-exam, mammography, and physical examinations. However, I would, and do, recommend the same diligent program to all women regardless of whether they take birth control pills or not.

Diet

A variety of studies looking at breast cancer incidences in the United States and other countries have pointed to an association between low-fat, high-fiber diets and lower breast cancer rates. Following a low-fat, low-cholesterol, and high-fiber diet will decrease your susceptibility to many other medical problems as well, such as heart disease, diabetes, gastrointestinitis, fatigue, and obesity. Ignoring the fact that a healthy diet can save your life is inviting trouble. The key role of diet in cancer prevention is brought into focus more clearly when you consider this: Studies have shown that a Japanese woman living in Japan (the Japanese being known for a diet which is practically fat-free) has approximately one eighth the risk of developing breast cancer as a Caucasian American woman. But when that Japanese woman moves to the United States, within one generation her female descendants have equally the same risk of developing breast cancer as their Caucasian counterparts.

A diet rich in natural vitamins A, B carotene, and C, may offer some degree of protection against breast cancer. Most medical experts will agree that the operative word here is *natural*. For some people, taking large doses of vitamin supplements can be very dangerous because of the body's inability to excrete these supplements in a safe, timely manner. The best way to get the vitamins your body needs is to get them naturally from foods such as broccoli, carrots, spinach, brussels sprouts, cabbage, cauliflower, tomatoes, sweet potatoes, green peppers, squash, apricots, oranges, strawberries, cantaloupe, lemons, and limes.

Fruits, vegetables, and bran are beneficial because of their high fiber content. The role of fiber in reducing the risk of heart attacks has been widely publicized.

I certainly don't have to tell you what components make up a healthy diet—you know. We all have to make our own choices. I am particularly careful about what I eat, for many reasons, the most important being the threat of a cancer recurrence. Still, I have learned to enjoy the life I have, and that includes an occasional glass of wine, hamburger, and dessert.

Smoking

Although there is no known link at this time between breast cancer and smoking, I cannot in all good conscience neglect to mention the detriments of this habit. It is the number-one cause of lung cancer deaths in the country, and lung cancer has surpassed breast cancer as the leading cause of cancer deaths in women. There are no advantages to smoking cigarettes. None.

Hormone Replacement Therapy

This is another issue of great controversy today. Before you can take a stand or ask your doctor where he stands, you need to know a little bit about hormone replacement therapy and what it could mean to your health.

The normal female menstrual cycle in premenopausal women involves the secretion of estrogens followed by progestins from the ovaries. This is followed by a building up and then shedding of the inner layer of the uterus, causing us to experience our monthly periods. As we enter menopause, our body stops producing these estrogens, a fact of life that comes naturally with the aging process. Along with menopause may come several unpleasant side effects such as hot flashes, irritability, and depression. Osteoporosis (the loss of calcium in the bones) is another common problem of women in or past menopause, causing a variety of problems including weak bones, painful fractures (particularly to the leg and hip), and loss of height.

Replacing the lost estrogens (estrogen replacement therapy, or ERT) can alleviate some or all of these problems. Some experts believe ERT is also effective in reducing the risk of cardiovascular disease. The controversy is this: While no one doubts ERT's potential value to women suffering from severe menopausal symptoms, many physicians feel it increases the risk of both breast cancer and cancer of the uterus (endometrial cancer). The latest scientific studies indicate that low doses of estrogen replacement treatment may be associated with a small increased risk of breast cancer. Estrogen replacement treatment by itself is also associated with a substantially increased risk of cancer of the uterus. As a means of rectifying the problem, adding a second group of hormones, progestins, to the therapy has been recommended. Studies indicate that by adding these low-dose progestins the risk of endometrial cancer is greatly reduced. But what about the risk of breast cancer? This is where the studies are most controversial. In the opinion of some experts, the adding of low-dose progestins to low-dose estrogens actually increases the risk of breast cancer. Other medical authorities disagree, saying that the studies do not indicate a heightened risk of breast cancer to women on estrogen replacement therapy in the vast majority of situations. They say that if there are breast cancer cells somewhere in your body that will ultimately show up as a recurrence, hormone replacement might affect the growth of those cells (either by speeding them up or slowing them down). These experts feel that receiving hormone replacement therapy is an informed-decision issue.

Clearly, there is still much to be learned in this area. Most experts will agree, however, that a woman with a personal history of breast cancer should be disease-free for at least five years before considering hormone replacement therapy for herself. Any woman considering this treatment option should discuss it thoroughly with her gynecologist. A former breast cancer patient should discuss it with her oncologist as well.

CHAPTER TWELVE

Gearing Up Again: If Cancer Recurs

When breast cancer is first diagnosed, most of us experience a plethora of emotions. Fright, anger, confusion, and desperation seem to take over in the beginning as the realization of our own mortality sinks in. As a woman learns more about her options and understands all that can be done to combat the disease, some of those emotions are replaced by hope and an overwhelming feeling of strength and determination. Ideally, she will get through the ordeal and will gain a better appreciation for life while living each new day to the fullest.

It doesn't always happen that way. After bravely enduring one or more types of treatment, even the most noble of fighters can be faced with the devastating news that her cancer has recurred. A recurring cancer is a tumor growth in the area of the original cancer site, either in the remaining breast tissue, the skin, the chest wall, or nearby lymph nodes. It may also be a form of metastasis, cancer that has spread through the blood and/or lymph system to other parts of the body such as the bones, liver, or brain. It is possible that some of the original cancer cells were not destroyed by the first round of treatment. They may have lain dormant for several months or even years before beginning a regrowth.

Having a breast cancer recurrence is not necessarily a death sentence. Many women go on to live full, healthy, and active lives after one or more cancer recurrences. Still, the emotional energy required to gear up again for more treatment after believing that you have beaten the disease can be staggering. A feeling of bitter disappointment combined with rage and despair can be crippling if you allow it to be. This is the time when you will need every bit of courage and positive energy you can muster. "Know, above all else, that this is not your fault," insists Dr. Jimmie Holland, chief of psychiatric services at Memorial Sloan-Kettering in New York. "Release the guilt. A cancer recurrence is not a personal failure, it is a disease."

The treatment options for breast cancer recurrence are the same as for initial breast cancer. If the initial surgery was less extensive, more surgery may be required. Chemotherapy, radiation therapy, and/or hormone therapy may also be suggested, although the dosages may vary according to your specific needs.

Should you be diagnosed with recurrent or metastatic disease, your medical team of experts as well as your emotional support system will need to come up with a new strategy and a new plan of action. Try to find strength in the fact that by now you are a much more knowledgeable and educated cancer patient. Some of the mystery and uncertainty about what to expect from the treatment will be diminished. Knowing what to expect will enable you to better organize your next round of treatment around the rest of your life.

And it is important to go on being as active as possible. Don't give up or give in to this disease. This time you may beat it—once and for all. Remember, others have done it successfully before you. If you do not know personally a patient who has survived recurrent or metastatic breast cancer, contact the Susan G. Komen Breast Cancer Foundation (see Resources, page 192), the National Cancer Institute (page 191), or the American Cancer Society (page 189); these organizations will be able to put you in touch with someone in your area who can give you, first-hand, the hope and courage you need to go on.

CHAPTER THIRTEEN

Joining the Race for the Cure

Nothing was ever accomplished by sitting around on your duff!

—ELLIE GOODMAN

The race for the cure is not the sole responsibility of medical professionals or cancer organizations like the Komen Foundation. The race will not be won until all women take part in it. At this time, there is no cure for breast cancer. But there *is* hope. *If breast cancer is detected in its earliest stages and treated promptly, there is a 95 percent survival rate.* When all women are made aware of the seriousness of breast cancer, the importance of early diagnosis, and the various treatment options, thousands more women's lives will be saved.

In taking the time to read this book, you have taken the first step in preparing yourself and those you love to run the race against breast cancer. Please, go a step further. Join with us: help save lives in your community. Give women what they need most—knowledge. Teach other women what you now know—*mammograms save lives.*

The Susan G. Komen Breast Cancer Foundation, in conjunction with the National Cancer Institute, has formulated a list of ways to successfully spread the word. If you have often wanted to do something for your community but didn't know where to begin, perhaps these suggestions will inspire you. Think how enriched your own life could be if you were partly responsible for helping save even one woman from suffering.

- Make a commitment. If you belong to a woman's organization, ask it to make a commitment to educating women about mammography. If you don't belong to an organization, call one that interests you and tell the leader of your idea—perhaps the PTA, a working women's group, your bowling league, tennis team, etc.

- Co-sponsor a "Women's Health Fair." Work with the local hospital, medical center, or cancer society to put on such an event. Arrange for local health care professionals to talk about the importance of mammography and to screen women at a low cost.
- Sponsor mammography education programs. Work with your employer or with other major employers in your area to sponsor mammography education programs. Suggest a women-only brown-bag-lunch seminar where local health care professionals can speak on mammography and breast self-examination.
- Work to extend insurance coverage of mammography. If your health coverage does not include screening mammograms, work with your company's employee insurance coordinator to extend your company's coverage to include this benefit.
- Ask your company's employee insurance coordinator to obtain resource lists from your insurer and make them available to all employees.
- Set up a bulletin board display. Develop a display of posters, brochures, and a list of local mammography facilities for your office, club, beauty salon, lingerie shop, department store, or grocery.
- Encourage the local broadcast media to run public service announcements. Prepared PSAs are available from the Susan G. Komen Breast Cancer Foundation (see Resources, page 192). Ask your local television stations, cable networks, and radio stations if they will play them.
- Inform the community about mammography facilities and costs. Survey local hospitals and freestanding mammography centers about their hours of availability and costs of services. Let your community know the results by writing a letter to the editor.
- Take a group of friends to get a mammogram. Borrow or rent a van and all go together. Then have lunch, see a movie—anything it takes to make the experience a pleasant one.
- Give the gift of mammography for Mother's Day, birthdays, or "Just Because" days.
- Ask for the gift of mammography from someone you love.
- Lobby your congressmen and senators to increase funding on the state and local level for mammography screening and breast cancer research. The federal budget has not kept up with the incidence of this disease.

CHAPTER FOURTEEN

And Now . . .

To love what you do and feel that it matters—how could anything be more fun?

—*KATHARINE GRAHAM*

Nine years after my original diagnosis, there is still a little panic that wells up inside me whenever it is time for a check-up. But I take a deep breath, say a little prayer, and go anyway. I do everything I know to keep healthy, and I really work hard at it. Still, I try not to forget to look up now and then and say, "Thanks."

Norman and I continue to cherish our life together and live every day to its fullest. Eric is sixteen years old and is, as always, the joy of my life. My parents, niece, nephew, and brother-in-law are working to rebuild their lives, living with the constant void of Suzy's absence.

The Susan G. Komen Breast Cancer Foundation is a nationwide organization with a fast-growing independent force of volunteers. We are enormously proud of the work we do and are beginning to see positive proof of our labor. This is an exciting time.

It is especially gratifying to me to see the problem of breast cancer slowly but surely making its way into the limelight. Eight years ago, no one would talk about this disease. Today it is "out of the closet," so to speak. This is largely due to the generosity of some of the country's most well-known celebrities, who have been willing to speak out on the cause. It is becoming fashionable to be informed about breast cancer.

I would like to see more of it. I would like to see still more funds being set aside nationally for breast cancer research and education. Since the Pap smear has been accepted as part of a woman's routine health check, the mortality rate for cervical cancer has decreased by 75 percent. I know the same could happen for breast cancer if women considered a mammogram part of a routine examination. I believe that if the entire medical community—including doctors, nurses, and patients—were to think in terms of preventive medicine rather than just curative medicine, more lives would be saved. Most people still only go to the doctor when they feel sick. Sometimes that is too late.

Ten years from now, when I see a significant improvement in the mortality rate for breast cancer, and I feel certain that I will, I will know that my sister is resting in peace because her final wishes have been fulfilled. We are winning. The victors are our mothers, our sisters, our daughters, our friends . . . ourselves.

A Breast Cancer Glossary

There are some terms you will see over and over again within this book and hear often in your doctor's office. I have tried to explain each term as it came up in the text, but I know from experience that "cancer talk" can sound like a foreign language at first. And foreign languages are easy to forget. The Susan G. Komen Breast Cancer Foundation has put together a quick reference list of common terms to refresh your memory at a glance. The definitions are short and uncomplicated, meant only to give you a fast, easy idea of what a word means. For more detailed information, use the index to find the term within the text, or ask your doctor.

Adjuvant Therapy: cancer treatment such as radiation or drugs (chemotherapy) used as a supplement to the primary form of treatment, which is surgery.

Alopecia: hair loss. Often occurs as a result of chemotherapy.

Anesthesia: entire or partial loss of feeling or sensation produced by drugs or gases.

Antiemetic: a medicine that prevents or relieves nausea and vomiting, used during chemotherapy.

Areola: the circular field of dark-colored skin surrounding the nipple.

Aspiration: withdrawal of fluid from a cyst with a hypodermic needle.

Axilla: the underarm area.

Benign: noncancerous (usually not life-threatening).

Biopsy: removal of suspicious tissue for examination under a microscope and diagnosis.

Excisional Biopsy: removal of an entire growth.
Fine Needle Aspirate: removal of cells with a needle and syringe.
Incisional Biopsy: removal of a section of a growth.
Needle Biopsy: removal of a plug of tissue using a needle.

Bone Scan: a way of taking pictures of the bones by injecting radioactive material into the bloodstream and witnessing the results with a special camera.

Bone (skeletal) Survey: X rays of the entire skeleton.

Breast Cancer: a potentially fatal tumor formed by the uncontrolled growth of abnormal breast cells that can invade and destroy surrounding tissue and can spread to other parts of the body. See METASTASIS.

Breast Implant: a round or tear-drop shaped sac inserted in the body to restore a breast form.

Breast Self-exam: the process in which women examine their own breasts every month in an effort to detect problems in an early stage.

CAT Scan: a sectional view of the entire body through X ray.

Chemotherapy: treatment with drugs to destroy cancer cells; often used to supplement surgery and/or radiation or to treat recurrent cancer.

Cyst: a fluid-filled mass, usually harmless, which can be removed by aspiration. See ASPIRATION.

Cytotoxic: cell-killing.

Diaphanography (DPG): a noninvasive procedure (a procedure that requires no cutting) which uses ordinary light as an investigative tool to detect breast masses; also called transillumination.

Diethylstilbestrol (DES): a female hormone which, when given artificially, has been linked with cancer growth.

Duct Ectasia: see MAMMARY DUCT ECTASIA.

Ductal Papillomas: small, noncancerous finger-like growths in the mammary ducts that cause a bloody nipple discharge. Commonly found in women forty-five to fifty.

Endocrine Manipulation: treating breast cancer by changing the hormonal balance of the body instead of using cell-killing drugs (chemotherapy).

Estrogen: a female hormone important to reproduction, which is produced by the ovaries and the adrenal glands and may be needed by some cancers for growth. See HORMONES.

Estrogen Receptor Assay (ERA): a test that must be done on cancerous tissue to see if a breast cancer is hormone-dependent and may be treated with hormone therapy.

Fat Necrosis: destruction of fat cells due to trauma or injury that can cause a noncancerous lump.

Fibroadenoma: a noncancerous, solid breast tumor most commonly found in younger women.

Fibrocystic Breast Condition: a noncancerous breast condition in which multiple cysts develop in one or both breasts. It can be accompanied by discomfort or pain that fluctuates with the menstrual cycle. Often called lumpy breasts.

Flow Cytometry: a test done on cancerous tissue that shows the aggressiveness of the tumor.

Frozen Section: a technique in which a part of the biopsy tissue is frozen immediately and a thin slice is then mounted on a microscope slide, enabling a pathologist to analyze it in just a few minutes for a diagnosis.

Galactocele: a clogged milk duct associated with child birth.

Halsted (Radical) Mastectomy: see MASTECTOMY.

Hormone Therapy: see ENDOCRINE MANIPULATION.

Hormones: substances made by the body that regulate the activity of certain cells or organs. They are largely responsible for reproductive function and aspects of appearance that distinguish the sexes.

Hormone Receptor Assay: a diagnostic test to determine whether a breast cancer's growth is influenced by hormones or can be treated with hormones.

Hysterectomy: surgical removal of the uterus.

Immunotherapy: treatment by modifying the body's immune defense system.

Infiltrating Duct Cell Cancer: a cancer that begins in the mammary ducts and spreads to surrounding tissue.

Intravenous (IV): entering the body by way of a vein.

Inverted Nipple: the turning inward of the nipple. Usually a congenital condition, but if it occurs where it has not previously existed, it can be a sign of breast cancer.

Linear Accelerator: a machine that produces high-energy X rays to destroy cancers.

Liver Scan: a way of visualizing the liver by injecting into the bloodstream a radioactive substance which lights up the organ during X ray.

Lump: any kind of abnormal mass in the breast (or elsewhere in the body).

Lumpy Breast Disease: see FIBROCYSTIC BREAST CONDITION.

Lumpectomy: a surgical procedure in which only the cancerous tumor and a ring of surrounding normal breast tissue are removed. Usually some of the underarm lymph nodes are removed at the same time. Also called tylectomy.

Lymph Nodes: bean-shaped filtering devices scattered along the vessels of the lymphatic system, which remove wastes and fluids from the body tissues and carry fluids that help the body fight infection. Those found in the underarm (axilla) are most likely to be invaded by breast cancer cells and so are often removed during breast cancer surgery.

Lymphedema: swelling in the arm caused by excess fluid that collects after lymph nodes and vessels are removed by surgery or damaged by X rays.

Magnetic Resonance Imaging (MRI): a magnet scan; a form of X ray using magnets instead of radiation. MRI gives a more clearly defined picture of fatty tissue than X ray.

Malignant: cancerous (life-threatening).

Mammary Duct Ectasia: a noncancerous breast disease most often found in women during menopause wherein the ducts in or beneath the nipples become clogged with fat, producing a lump.

Mammary Glands: the breast glands that produce and carry milk, by way of the mammary ducts, to the nipples during pregnancy and breast-feeding.

Mammography/Mammogram: an X ray of the breast that can detect tumors before they can be felt.

Baseline Screening Mammogram: a mammogram performed on healthy breasts, to establish a basis for comparison later.

Mastectomy: surgical removal of the breast and some surrounding tissue.

Modified Radical Mastectomy: the most common type of mastectomy performed today. The breast, breast skin, nipple, areola, and underarm lymph nodes are removed, while the chest muscles are saved.

Prophylactic Mastectomy: a procedure sometimes recommended for patients at very high risk for developing cancer in one or both breasts. *Subcutaneous mastectomy,* done before cancer is detected, removes the breast tissue but leaves the outer skin, areola, and nipple intact. (This is not a suitable cancer operation.)

Radical Mastectomy (Halsted Radical): the surgical removal of the breast, breast skin, nipple, areola, chest muscles, and underarm lymph nodes. Rarely done today.

Segmental Mastectomy (Partial Mastectomy): a surgical procedure in which only a portion of the breast is removed, including the cancer and a surrounding margin of healthy breast tissue. See also LUMPECTOMY.

Menopause: the time in a woman's life when the menstrual cycle ends and the ovaries produce lower levels of hormones. Usually occurs between the ages of forty-five and fifty-five.

Metastasis: the spread of cancer from one part of the body to another through the lymphatic system or the bloodstream. The cells in the new cancer location are the same type as those in the original site.

Medical Oncologist: a physician who specializes in the diagnosis and treatment of cancer and may prescribe chemotherapy, arrange for radiation therapy, or refer a patient to a surgeon or other specialist.

One-Step Procedure: a procedure in which a surgical biopsy is performed under general anesthesia and, if cancer is found, a mastectomy or lumpectomy is done immediately, as part of the same operation.

Oophorectomy: surgical removal of the ovaries, sometimes performed as a part of hormone therapy. See also ENDOCRINE MANIPULATION.

Palliative Therapy: a treatment that may relieve symptoms without curing the disease, such as drugs that relieve nausea (see ANTIEMETICS) and radiation given for pain control.

Partial Mastectomy: see MASTECTOMY.

Pathologist: a physician with special training in diagnosing diseases from samples of tissues.

Palpation: examining the breasts by feel, with the hands.

Permanent Section: a technique in which a thin slice of biopsy tissue is mounted on a slide to be examined under a microscope by a pathologist in order to establish a diagnosis. Usually takes three days for results.

Progesterone Receptor Assay (PRA): a test that must be done on cancerous tissue to see if a breast cancer is hormone-dependent and can be treated by hormone therapy. Used as a check on the results of the ESTROGEN RECEPTOR ASSAY.

Prosthesis: an artificial limb or form. In the case of breast cancer, a breast form that can be worn under clothing after a mastectomy.

Radiation Therapy: treatment with high-energy X rays to destroy cancer cells. Used to supplement surgery.

Radiation Oncologist: a physician specifically trained in the use of high-energy X rays to treat cancer.

Radiologist: a physician who specializes in diagnosis of diseases by the use of X rays.

Reconstruction: a way to recreate the breast's shape after a natural breast has been removed; various surgical procedures are available. Sometimes performed immediately (at the time of mastectomy) but usually delayed several months or years.

Recurrence: reappearance of cancer at the same site (local), near the site (regional), or in other areas of the body (metastatic).

Silicone Gel: medical-grade silicone rubber in gel form that is similar to the fluid qualities of the normal breast and is used for implants.

Staging: certain tests and examinations that should be done before any type of definitive treatment is decided upon to determine the site of the tumor, whether the lymph nodes are involved, and if the cancer has spread through the bloodstream or the lymphatic system (metastasized). Four definite stages are used to describe the progress of the disease.

Tumor: an abnormal growth or mass of tissue; can be either cancerous or noncancerous.

Two-Step Procedure: when surgical biopsy and breast surgery are performed in two separate stages. Compare ONE-STEP PROCEDURE.

Tylectomy: see LUMPECTOMY.

Ultrasonography/Ultrasound: a noninvasive procedure (a procedure that does not require cutting into the skin) using a sound-wave imaging technique to examine a part of the body, or to further evaluate a breast lump or other abnormalities seen on a mammogram. Also used to evaluate the liver.

X rays: electromagnetic radiations which can, at low levels, produce images that can diagnose cancer and, at high levels, destroy cancer cells.

Index

ACR, *see* American College of Radiology
ACS, *see* American Cancer Society
actinomycin D, 133
adjuvant therapy, 30, 43, 100, 106, 159
adolescence, breast development in, 63, 65, 67
Adriamycin (doxorubicin hydrochloride), 46, 111, 133
age, aging:
  breasts and, 67, 121
  cancer and, 45, 74, 148
  mammography and, 74
  premature, 133
  in treatment, 100
AIDS, 63, 134–35
alcohol, chemotherapy and, 52
Alkeran (melphalan), 111
alkylating agents, 111
all-fruit diet, 118
alopecia, *see* hair thinning, hair loss
alternative therapy, 118–20
AMA (American Medical Association), 91
American Cancer Society (ACS), 70, 74, 84, 122, 136, 147
American College of Radiology (ACR), 75
American College of Surgeons, 92
American Medical Association (AMA), 91
American Osteopathic Board of Radiology, 75
American Society of Clinical Oncology, 36, 91
American Society of Plastic and Reconstructive Surgeons, 122

Ames, Fred, 55
  Nancy's partnership with, 40, 42, 43, 45, 46, 92
aminoglutethamide, 114
analgesics, 77
anesthesia, 108, 159, 163
aneuploidy, 88
anger, strength provided by, 18
antibiotics, 56, 111
antidepressants, 50
antiemetics, 159, 164
antimetabolites, 111
appearance, 43, 48, 50–51, 129–38
  exercise and, 56, 65, 129, 136–38, 141
  hats and, 130, 132
  makeup and, 49, 129, 130, 134–35, 138
  publications on, 130
  scarves and, 50, 130, 132, 135
  of skin, *see* skin
  and successful treatment, 129–30
  wardrobe and, 50, 121, 129–30, 132, 135–36, 138
  wigs and, *see* wigs
areola, 66, 159
  in reconstructive surgery, 124, 128
aspiration, needle, 26, 84, 86, 159, 160
A team, *see* support team
axillary lymph nodes, *see* underarm lymph nodes

back muscles in reconstructive surgery, 125
Barton, Fritz, 92
baseline mammogram, 74, 163

Our's is the winning battle, the victors are our mothers, our sisters, our daughters, our friends . . . ourselves.

Your Role in the Susan G. Komen Breast Cancer Foundation

The primary mission of The Susan G. Komen Breast Cancer Foundation is to achieve higher recovery rates for breast-cancer victims by advancing education, treatment, and research.

Early detection is the most ethical and cost effective approach to breast cancer until a cure or control can be found. The Komen Foundation sponsors education seminars to help women understand the importance of screening and to cope when the disease has been diagnosed.

The Komen Foundation educated the public to support landmark legislation in Texas for mandatory insurance coverage of screening mammograms for women thirty-five and over; since 1987, thirty-three other states have followed that lead. The Komen Foundation advocates informed decision legislation, screening vans for the indigent and medically underserved and for quality control at mammography facilities.

The Komen RACE FOR THE CURE™ is a unique all-women's event: conceived, designed, and implemented by The Susan G. Komen Breast Cancer Foundation to promote positive awareness, education, and early detection of breast cancer. There are many national groups raising money to fund cancer causes, but few specifically devoted to breast cancer and none with an event more inspiring than RACE FOR THE CURE™.

Originating in Dallas in 1983, the Race has grown to include eighteen sites in cities across America from San Francisco to New York. Race sites include: Austin, TX; Wichita, KS; Peoria, IL; Philadelphia, PA; Plano, TX; Davenport, IA, Washington, D.C.; Decatur, IL; Aspen, CO; Amarillo, TX; Houston, TX; New York City, NY; Dallas, TX; Atlanta, GA; San Francisco, CA; and Scranton, PA.

The RACE FOR THE CURE™ series has been nationally recognized as a premier sporting event by *Runner's World* and *Running Times* magazines. But the most significant contribution it makes is to screening the medically underserved in each commuinity. Because of the event, thousands of women who could not afford mammograms are being screened (through grants made to local ACR-accredited screening facilities) and are being taught breast self-exam.

The Komen RACE FOR THE CURE™ has proved to be an enormously effective way to reach many, many women with the message that breast cancer is not necessarily fatal if mammography and breast self-exam become routine. As well as being a road race for serious runners, an emotionally charged event which attracts many first-timers and recreational runners, it is an opportunity for thousands of women, running or walking with the names of dead loved ones on their backs, to send the breast-cancer message to their communities. Marilyn Tucker Quayle is National Honorary Chairman of the RACE FOR THE CURE™ Series.

One of the foundation's projects has been to fund screening centers for women from all walks of life at both private and public hospitals. It is estimated that over 100,000 women have had a mammogram at a Susan G. Komen Breast Center affiliate. A network of Susan G. Komen Breast Cancer Screening Centers is being set up across the country. Women need mammography to be affordable and accessible. The screening centers (which may include vans to serve rural areas) will be located conveniently and operated in a cost efficient manner.

The population—women, their significant others, physicians, and other health professionals—need to understand the importance of early detection. Every center will have an education component that will attempt to not only inform, but to also change behavior.

Having a low-quality mammogram, which may create a false sense of assurance or which may recommend unnecessary diagnostic procedures, is worse than not being screened at all. The Komen Centers will be required to be accredited by the American College of Radiology (ACR) and will be monitored for compliance with internal guidelines.

Research holds the key to the cure of this devastating disease. Each affiliate will gather data for research projects and will contribute resources to the foundation's national research programs.

In 1987, the Komen Alliance was established in Dallas, Texas to provide a superior education program designed to strengthen the understanding and practice of prevention, diagnostic, and treatment methods created for patients and their families, physicians and other health care providers. A team of specialists conducts ongoing research to determine causes and improve treatment of breast diseases. Through this organization, the most advanced possible therapy, both classical and experimental, are made readily available to women with breast disease. The Komen Alliance draws on a national network of talent, commitment and resources to battle breast cancer.

The Foundation has raised over $9,000,000 to support basic science and clinical research projects at some of the finest breast cancer research laboratories across the country including: University Of Illinois, Urbana-Champaign, IL; National Cancer Institute, Bethesda, MD; Lombardi Cancer Institute, Washington, DC; The Peralta Cancer Research Institute, Oakland, CA; Geraldine Brush Cancer Research Institute, Oakland, CA; The Komen Alliance, Dallas, TX; M.D. Anderson, Houston, TX; University of Texas Southwestern Medical Center, Dallas, TX; University of Texas Health Science Center, San Antonio, TX; Johns Hopkins, Baltimore, MD; Lineberger Research Center, Chapel Hill, NC; Greater Southeast Community Hospital, Washington, D.C., University of California, San Francisco, CA.

WE NEED YOU. . . .

The Susan G. Komen Breast Cancer Foundation is battling a formidable enemy, one that's gaining momentum. We're not fighting for principle . . . not for an obscure cause.

**We're Fighting for
Our Very Lives. But To Win
We Need You To Join Our Battle.**

Through educating yourself about the disease, taking preventive measures, volunteering to help our battle or contributing . . . we need you!

If you need further information about breast cancer, please call: 1-800-I'M-AWARE (1-800-462-9273).

To learn how you can volunteer in your neighborhood or further help us in our fight, please write:

The Susan G. Komen Breast Cancer Foundation
6820 LBJ Freeway, Suite 130
Dallas, Texas 75240
(214) 980-8841.

Notes